Papers of the
British Association for Korean Studies

Volume 11

Papers of the British Association for Korean Studies

Editor: SUSAN PARES

The editorial office of the *Papers of the British Association for Korean Studies* is at 86 Crescent Lane, London SW4 9PL, UK. Email address: spares@myway.com

Publication of volume 11 of the *Papers of the British Association for Korean Studies* is made possible with financial assistance from the Korea Foundation and with the support of the Embassy of the Republic of Korea in London, of the University of Sheffield, and of the British Museum, London. BAKS once again extends sincere thanks to John Cayley of Wellsweep for his assistance with the cover design.

All volumes of the *Papers* are available for purchase through the BBR Academic Bookshop (http://www.bbr-online.com/academic). For membership forms and current announcements, visit the website of the British Association for Korean Studies (http://www.dur.ac.uk/BAKS).

ISBN 1-872588-17-4 • ISSN 0965-1942

Copyright © 2007 by the British Association for Korean Studies.

CONTENTS

KEYNOTE ADDRESS

MARGARET DRABBLE   1
    The writing of *The Red Queen* (2006 BAKS Conference)

PAPERS

SOWON S. PARK   7
    Metempsychosis and chiasmatic encounters: on Margaret
    Drabble's *The Red Queen* (2006 BAKS Conference)

KEITH PRATT   19
    The evolution of museums in the ROK (2005 BAKS Study day)

DON STARR   33
    The World Koreanists Forum 2005 and Korean studies
    (2005 BAKS Study day)

ANDREW KILLICK   49
    Hwang Byungki and North-South musical exchange
    (2005 BAKS Study day)

DAVID LAKIN   57
    The Kaesŏng archaeological project (2005 BAKS Study day)

KEITH BENNETT   65
    Bamboo curtain or open door? Challenges and opportunities
    of the DPRK: Perspectives of a business consultant
    (2005 BAKS Study day)

NICK BONNER   73
    The use of informal diplomacy and cultural exchanges in the DPRK
    (2005 BAKS Study day)

CONTRIBUTORS TO *BAKS 11*   81

CORRECTION TO *BAKS 10*   82

EDITOR'S NOTE

This latest volume of BAKS *Papers* presents contributions from the BAKS Study day held in December 2005 at the British Museum on the theme of 'Informal diplomacy and the Korean peninsula'; and a couple of papers from the September 2006 BAKS Conference organised by the University of Sheffield. These two papers continue the subject of the 2005 Study day, and for that reason the editor has preferred to group them with the earlier pieces.

'Informal diplomacy' can take many guises and be conducted across many fields. The organisers of the 2005 Study day set no precise boundaries and let the concept of non-official contacts roam from inter-Korean relations to dealings between either Korea and the outside world. The aim was to see where the subject-matter led and how a particular activity complemented formal diplomacy—or ran separately from it, and to get some flavour of the wide range of informal relations.

The first example is, in a sense, the most personal and the most engaged. Margaret Drabble, in the keynote address to the 2006 Conference, told us something of the processes, and difficulties, of writing her novel *The Red Queen* (published in 2004). It is a stimulating exposition of the creative demands imposed by writing but also by the business of entering into another cultural and literary tradition. The reactions of some Koreans to her efforts were hostile, but Sowon Park, in her companion piece, elucidates the key concepts of the novel.

The next two papers, by Keith Pratt and Don Starr, discuss two areas, museums and Korean studies, where official Korean concern with the presentation of essential elements in (in this instance) South Korean culture is closely intertwined with what domestic and foreign players might seek. Andrew Killick follows these papers with an examination of the tentative and circumscribed efforts of North and South Koreans to engage with each other in the field of music. David Lakin next describes the attempts of a Western international group to work with North Korean authorities in investigating the archaeological wealth of Kaesŏng. Keith Bennett then analyses some of the challenges involved in doing business with North Korea; and Nick Bonner outlines his and his colleagues' drive to engage with the North Koreans in tourist and cultural exchanges.

Where possible, romanisation has followed the standards for Korean current in academic circles, that is, McCune-Reischauer, the current standard for Japanese—Hepburn—and pinyin romanisation for Chinese. Exceptions to the McCune-

Reischauer system are some proper names and instances of the North Korean style of romanisation. The editor has followed the practice of italicising specialised words only on their first appearance in a text and thereafter presenting them in ordinary roman typeface.

BAKS is indebted to the Korea Foundation for a generous financial donation towards the costs of printing. As ever, BAKS thanks the Embassy of the Republic of Korea, its Cultural Section and especially Mr Sung In-Joon, Minister-Counsellor in the Embassy, for support. It is grateful too for the support it has received from the Centre for Korean Studies of the School of East Asian Studies, University of Sheffield, and from the British Museum.

Susan Pares
London, February 2007

KEYNOTE ADDRESS

THE WRITING OF *THE RED QUEEN*

MARGARET DRABBLE

This paper is an attempt to explain what compelled me to embark on the foolhardy enterprise of trying to write a novel inspired by my reading of the memoirs of Lady Hong, the Crown Princess, and why the novel took the form it did. This project was fraught with difficulties, and I am grateful for an opportunity to try to explain myself.

My first disclaimer and my first apology concern my difficulty with pronouncing and even memorising the names of the historical characters of the memoirs. I know that the Korean memoir is called the *Han Joong Nok*,[*] and that this title is familiar to all Koreans, but to me this remains the very first enigma. Being entirely self taught in anything to do with Korea, I do not even know how to pronounce the syllables of *Han Joong Nok*, and I know that their meaning has been translated variously. I have few sounds in my head to accompany my readings of Korean works in translation, no classroom knowledge of the language, no conversational experience. I have now been to Korea three times, and I have tried to supply my deficiencies by watching Korean films, but I am a poor linguist, and too old to learn much. It is too late for me to learn a new language. So why, you may well wonder, did I take the great risk of trying to use Lady Hong's memoirs as a starting point for a work of fiction?

I first came across this work, in an excellent translation by Professor Haboush published by the University of California Press, in the year 2000. I had been invited to a conference about the globalisation of literature in Seoul, sponsored by the Daesan Foundation, entitled 'Crossing the boundaries: literature in the multicultural world'. I was scheduled to speak on post-colonial literature from a British perspective. Before I left for Seoul, I did a little homework about my destination, and talked to a few scholars, one of whom loaned me her copy of the memoirs. I did not read it before I went, but I read it soon after my return, when images from Korea and curiosity about its history were still fresh in my mind. And I was completely transfixed by it. It had an overpowering effect on me. I was gripped by this narrative of intrigue and violence and survival, which seemed to me to have a Shakespearean tragic power. It leaped

---

[*] *Ed.* Also romanised as *Hanjung rok*.

across the borders of time and space, from past to present, from East to West. I felt as though I were reading *Hamlet* or *Macbeth* for the first time, without knowing the ending. The story unfolded for me with obsessive power, and would not leave me. I felt it belonged uniquely both to its writer, and to the world. It was a universal drama. How could this be, when its author during her long life was virtually imprisoned within the palace compound? How had she managed to communicate so directly with a reader who knew nothing of the culture in which she had lived? My novel explores these issues, and attempts to discuss the proposition of the possibility of universal human nature, and of the universal story.

I think the idea of writing a novel based on this theme came to me when I was re-telling the princess's story to an old friend of mine, a sociologist, with a particular interest in memoir, life-writing and autobiography. We were walking along a river bank together, and eventually we sat down on a rock by the water to finish the tale, and she then cross-questioned me about the narrative techniques, the point of view, the overlapping versions of Lady Hong's life, her purpose in writing. And I noticed that in re-telling the story, although I had given full value to the horror and pathos and violence of the events of two hundred years earlier, I had also been questioning the narrator's account from a contemporary perspective. What would Lady Hong have felt now about these events, and about women's lives, and what had changed in history—and, as importantly, what had not changed? I felt I had a theme which was demanding my attention, a character who was asking for another voice.

I told my friend about the way in which Lady Hong mentions that when she was a child she envied her cousin's red silk skirt. That little splash of colour illumines her narration brilliantly. It is a stroke of narrative genius. Why did she mention it? Did she know that it would authenticate her voice and her witness for centuries to come?

(Some readers have objected to my stating, in my novel, that Lady Hong 'envied' her cousin, and indeed in her own account she does insist that she was not envious: but one of the most intriguing aspects of her narrative style is the way in which her insistence at times suggests its opposite. She protests too much. She tells us repeatedly of her respect for her father-in-law the king, but it is not always respect that emerges from her summary of events. She was a very shrewd observer, and a very careful recorder, writing in dangerous times: an unreliable narrator, who cannot always tell the facts as they are, and it was my sense that many of her statements needed de-coding, and would have been de-coded by her contemporaries, who were very familiar with courtly language and courtly euphemisms.)

Reading this first translation was only the beginning of my quest. There are two other translations, both of which I read, and I also read as much contemporary material as I could find (including some very fine poems of the period available in English). I read histories, and searched data bases, and visited galleries and exhibitions and lectures, and became a member of BAKS. Of course my study was superficial—how could it not be?—but it gave me great pleasure. I remember with particular pleasure a visit to the Musée Guimet in Paris in 2002 to see an exhibition of paintings and screens—this was an indulgence, and a delight. The catalogue is one of my treasures. (I particularly loved the *chaekkori* paintings, and one of them, which shows a vase of peonies and a pair of glasses open on a book, was a direct inspiration for my bespectacled 20th-century heroine, Barbara Halliwell.) I revisited Seoul, to see the palace where the princess had been immured for nearly the whole of her adult life, and I walked round the walls of Suwŏn. The mingling of past and present in Korea today—its extraordinary visual mix of ancient and super-modern—became part of my theme. I was by this stage in mid-novel, and had realised that what I was working on was a transcultural novel, a novel which would raise questions about cultural relativism, essentialism, female narrative, family dynamics, evolutionary biology and the universality (or not) of the Oedipus complex. One of my models was Mark Twain's time-travel fantasy *A Connecticut Yankee at King Arthur's Court* (1889), with its darkly comic double-take on American capitalism and Camelot chivalry. My crown princess would look at the death penalty in the United States and the abuse of the Hippocratic oath in Britain with the hindsight of two hundred years of history, and pronounce her damning verdict on progress. We have moved on in some ways—in others, not at all. The casuistry surrounding the manner of the death of the Crown Prince I found particularly fascinating, as it seemed to echo some of the more elaborate objections that we hear today about the right to assisted suicide and voluntary euthanasia. I was unfortunately obliged to remove some of this material from my novel, because of copyright difficulties with material from another source, and I regret that.

My character Dr Halliwell is a strong opponent of the death penalty, and so am I. I wished to make the point that the United States, which prides itself on its civilised and progressive values, still executed minors and the criminally insane. I was using the story of the horrible death of the Crown Prince to illustrate the fact that we in the West have not progressed very much.

(In fact, the US law on executing minors convicted of a capital offence while under age has in the past months been successfully challenged by the Supreme Court of the US—I would like to think *The Red Queen* contributed to this change of heart, but I think that would be claiming too much!).

I have mentioned the word 'copyright', and must devote a minute or two to this very vexed matter. I had been aware from the beginning of the dangers of accusations of cultural appropriation—dangers which were an integral part of my theme, and part of the attraction of it. Being aware, I proceeded, as I thought, in a correct manner, contacting the most recent and most scholarly translator and through her the American publishers, and declaring my interest. We met, and, as I thought, came to an agreement. I naturally offered to pay for use of any copyright material, and also suggested the inclusion of a Foreword or Afterword written by her which could place my fictional efforts in a critical context. I envisaged, with what now seems like a childish naiveté, the possibility of shared platforms, public discussions, collaborative debates, joint publicity, mutual encouragement. I still feel that it ought to be possible to come to some friendly accommodation. In an ideal world, could it not be possible to produce a joint publication, of the original *Han Joong Nok* in English, with my fictionalised version in the same volume? Then the reader could contrast and compare and come to her own conclusions. I also think it would be immensely interesting for the general reader if Professor Haboush's *The Memoirs of Lady Hyegyong: The Autobiographical Writings of a Crown Princess of Eighteenth Century Korea* (1995) could be amalgamated with the some of the material about the death of Prince Sado from her volume *A Heritage of Kings: One Man's Monarchy in the Confucian World* (1988), and published by the same publisher in one imprint. These histories belong together, and it seems a pity to me that they cannot appear together.

To cut a long story short, when I sought approval for the first draft of my novel I ran into accusations of Orientalism and cultural appropriation, of "egregious error" and cynicism and plagiarism and ignorance. *The Red Queen*, it seemed, was full of crimes, the least of which was a reference to Korea in the 18th century as a frozen land and, by implication, a 'hermit kingdom'. This latter phrase has been used by Koreans and Westerners for centuries, referring to the Chosŏn dynasty's undisputed policy of isolationism, but it is, I was told, no longer correct. We are now to believe that the Koreans never were and are not now hermits. They welcome cultural interchange and debate.

Nevertheless, the phrase 'hermit kingdom' was not to be used by me.

But it was the question of breach of copyright that frightened my publishers, and led to my revising my text—some of it for the better, some to its loss. Some passages have gone forever, and not even I now know where they are. This is a very complex matter, and the legal issues are not quite of the dimensions of those that surrounded Dan Brown and the *Da Vinci Code*, but they were not dissimilar. What copyright can be held in the translation of a factual narrative by a real woman who died in 1815? This question is not as simple to answer as I thought it was.

Clearly, I have no access to any of the original extant versions of the *Han Joong Nok*, and indeed I have forgotten how many survive, though I was once quite well informed about these texts. All I had to work with were three English versions, compiled and arranged from these overlapping texts. These vary very substantially in many ways, and I cannot judge the authenticity of any of them. All I can tell is what rings true to me as a reader, or what is of interest to me as a writer. Let me look, briefly, at a key moment in Prince Sado's life, a moment that was essential to my interpretation of the three principal characters of the psychodrama—the king, his son, and Lady Hong. It is one of the most remarkable moments in the entire work. It is the moment at which the Crown Prince turns on his father, in an attempt to explain his own violent behaviour. This is my own version:

> According to Prince Sado, his father now asked him directly about the killings, and, being unable to lie to his father, Sado confessed to them. According to King Yŏngjo, however, Sado began to speak of them of his own accord, believing his father knew all about them anyway. I do not know which of these versions is more accurate. Whoever spoke first, the outcome was the same.
>
> Prince Sado explained himself to his father in these words:
> "It relieves my suppressed anger, sir, to kill people or animals."
> "Why is your anger aroused?"
> "Because I am so hurt."
> "Why are you so hurt?"
> "Because you do not love me, and also I am terrified of you because you constantly reproach and censure me. These are the causes of my illness."
>
> Then, by both their accounts, Sado began to outline the killings—of eunuchs, attendants, prostitutes, ladies-in-waiting—and his father listened to this catalogue of crimes in horrified silence.
>
> (*The Red Queen*, 2004. Hardback edition, Viking:91–92)

This interchange is obviously crucial to my interpretation of Lady Hong's story, and one of the clues to its impact on me. Her recounting of this incident, and the emphasis she places on it, reveal her extraordinary insight into her husband's state of mind. When I ran into copyright objections, I became very anxious that this passage would prove unique to the version which I had been forbidden even to paraphrase. So it was with much relief that I checked with the other versions in English and discovered that the wording in all three (and in my fourth version) was almost identical. This gave me permission to use the episode, but also, I believe, indicated that these were the very words that the prince and the king used. It is a true moment of witness.

Questions of translation and mistranslation, of interpretation and misinterpretation and reinterpretation, are of perennial interest. In my post-modern novel, I clearly made use of time travel, ghostly narration, and ghostly coincidence, and deliberate anachronism. But I freely admit that I also made some unforced errors, which I tried to correct in the paperback version of 2005—for example, "brown polished floor boards" on p. 54, have become "smooth oiled stone slabs", in response to several complaints from readers.

Lady Hong does not haunt me as she did while I was writing this novel, but I have by no means lost interest in her, she has a busy and continuing after-life. I gather she has many real-life descendants. Korean novelist Hwang Seok-Young told me that he knows family members alive today, and Chicago-based novelist and journalist Euny Hong has written a very racy novel called *My Blue Blood: A Comedy of Sex and*

Manners, published this year (2006), which takes far more liberties with the Hongs than I ever dared to do.

One last thought: several thoughtful readers have questioned my choice of a genre that I call in my subtitle 'tragicomedy'. The original story is tragic: why introduce any comic element? I am not sure I can give a very good answer. The tone introduced itself. Maybe the long dead see life as more ridiculous than the living. Or maybe some forms of violence and excess can be approached only through a satiric distance. Listening to the radio the other evening, I heard a discussion of Shostakovich's opera *Lady Macbeth of Mtsensk*, in which the composer was said to have described his work as a 'satiric tragedy'. I though that a very striking phrase, and wish I had thought of it myself. It seems apposite to the story I was trying to tell.

Bibliography

Drabble, Margaret, 2004. *The Red Queen: A Transcultural Tragicomedy*. London: Viking. [Paperback editions: QPD, 2004; London: Penguin Books Ltd., 2005]

Haboush, JaHyun Kim, 1988. *A Heritage of Kings: One Man's Monarchy in the Confucian World*. Studies in Oriental Culture, No. 21. New York: Columbia University Press

Hyegyonggung Hong Ssi. *Han Joong Nok: Reminiscences in Retirement: Crown Princess Hong*. Translated by Bruce C. Grant and Kim Chin-man, 1980. New York: Larchwood Publications

——. *Memoirs of a Korean Queen, by 'Lady Hong'*. Edited, introduced and translated by Yang-hi Choe-Wall, 1985. London; New York: KPI Ltd

——. *The Memoirs of Lady Hyegyong: The Autobiographical Writings of a Crown Princess of Eighteenth Century Korea*. Edited, translated and annotated by JaHyun Kim Haboush, 1995. Berkeley: University of California Press

PAPERS

METEMPSYCHOSIS AND CHIASMATIC ENCOUNTERS: ON MARGARET DRABBLE'S *THE RED QUEEN*

SOWON S. PARK

In *You Always Remember the First Time*, a volume of stories edited by the avant-garde writer B. S. Johnson, story 19 begins with a nineteen-year-old English boy on his National Service, in search of a radical departure from home.[1]

> Returning to Catterick Camp after being sick-on-leave with tonsillitis I discovered they'd put me down for a 'Home' posting. Immediately I dashed along to the RSM's office and complained that I wanted to go overseas.
> "It's a bit late. Where did you want to go?"
> "To Korea," I said.
> "Good God! Why?"
> "To get as far away from England as possible."

The officer's response, "Good God! Why?" encapsulates a typical British attitude to Korea which reaches far beyond the confines of this narrative. As late as 1975, when this volume was published, Korea was, for most British people, the farthest point on earth; and if this was not factually correct, it was nevertheless true for the cultural consciousness of the British people.

So when the news came that Margaret Drabble was writing a novel based on a Korean classic, Lady Hyegyŏng's *Hanjung rok*, the Korean expatriate community in Britain expressed as much amazement as delight. And in the context of what has been happening with regards to Korean popular culture in the last decade, wild speculations were rife: is the famous Hallyu reaching the shores of Britain? Was Lady Hyegyŏng to be re-born as a highbrow Hallyu star to join ranks with Yon Sama and Rain?[2] Drabble is not an author one associates with the Far East, let alone the Neo-Confucian, faction-riven court of 18th-century Chosŏn (1392–1910). Rather, her work to date has been strongly associated with the British intellectual bourgeoisie she has represented over the last four decades. Her chronicles of the social, economic and political texture of contemporary British life, more often than not portrayed from a woman's viewpoint, are so sociologically exact that if one wanted to discover for oneself what it is like actually to live in Britain without doing so, or if a future sociologist wanted to immerse him- or herself in British life of the latter half of the 20th century, the quickest route would be to read her 'condition of England' novels, *The Realms of Gold* (1975) or *The Ice Age* (1977). One might turn to these in the same way one might turn to Arnold Bennett for a segment of Edwardian life, or to Trollope for a slice of Victorian. Thus it was a tonic and a challenge to learn that a writer who typifies Englishness travelled two hundred years and half-way across the globe for her latest literary enterprise, her sixteenth novel, not representing England abroad, but representing Korea to England.

It was a challenge because popular representations of Korea in Britain, so far, have tended to gravitate towards fixed poles of sensationalism and utility. The sensationalist pole obliges any representation of Korea to be on the level of *kimchi* and dog-munching axis of evil, implicitly underlining that Korea is the back of beyond, too remote and not attention-grabbing enough to pursue on its own terms; and the pole of utility confines it to the sober pages of *The Economist* and *The Financial Times*. On the rare occasion that Korea is represented culturally, it tends to be described in terms of other more familiar places, often in quite a bewildering array of similes. For example, in 2005, in the pages of *The Guardian,* Seoul was dubbed the 'New Tokyo' and then, a few paragraphs down, 'Bangkok on Steroids' and then finally, an 'oriental version of Birmingham'.[3] Two decades ago, Korea was grouped as one of the 'little tigers' or NICs; then it was one of the countries benefiting, economically or politically, from 'Asian values'. As Perry Anderson noted in 1996, Korea is left in a vague limbo of acronyms and bestiaries compared with the dominating images of China and Japan.[4] One can reasonably infer from all this that the concept of Korea is just beyond the mental reach of the average British reader, and that Korea in the British imagination to say the least is blurry, out-of-focus, in-between.

The Red Queen (2004)[5] is a culmination as well as a major departure from previous representations of Korea in Britain. Partly set in Chosŏn, *The Red Queen* is a variation on, and a homage to, *Hanjung rok*, the four memoirs of Lady Hyegyŏng (1735–1815), wife of Crown Prince Sado, the tragic 'mad' prince who was the son of the Great King Yŏngjo and the father of the Great King Chŏngjo— the two Sage monarchs of Chosŏn.[6] It is a major departure, not only and obviously from sketchy journalistic reports but from earlier anthropological or sociological representations of Korea, reflecting as it does the rapidity with which associated areas of concern to post-colonial literature have been brought into the centre of British literary discourse. Unlike, for example Isabella Bird Bishop's *Korea and her Neighbours* (1897),[7] to which Drabble pays tribute in the novel, *The Red Queen* is informed by issues of power relations that are at work when ethnic or cultural differences are represented. While Bishop approached Korean culture as an object of empirical knowledge to be understood in terms of existing European thought, Drabble problematises ethnocentricity while at the same time asserting the need to find "universal transcultural human characteristics".[8] So Drabble pursues ideas of common universal experiences by juxtaposing the 18th-century Chosŏn court with 20th-century Western sensibilities, proposing in the process a different and more potent model of cultural exchange. What is attempted is no less than a true cross-cultural enterprise—a chiasmatic encounter: a real interchange of cultures where the gaps between the two are crossed but then crossed again in a chiasma, relating to the ancient Greek word for cross, where two things intertwine and form an intersection in the form of the letter 'x'.

Hanjung rok

The Red Queen, as Drabble states, is the "fifth" memoir to the existing four by Lady Hyegyŏng. Therefore it seems necessary to examine the original texts in order to provide some context for this additional piece. The title *Hanjung rok* can be interpreted as 'Records made in tranquillity' or 'Records made in distress', depending on whether one sees 'Han' as the Chinese character 閑 or 恨. As one can deduce from this, *Hanjung rok* was written in Korean (*hangŭl*), which was devised in the mid-15th century. At that time, all discourse in the public sphere was written in Chinese, but it was customary for women to write in hangŭl. And though men did occasionally write in hangŭl in private, for example, when writing letters addressed to women, most of the documents of this period, like the *Sillok*, are in Chinese.[9] *Hanjung rok* is an exceptional text because though other records of the Crown Prince Sado exist in great numbers, this account is written in a more personal language and gives a relatively more intimate account of the series of events, and thus appears more modern to contemporary readers and is certainly far more accessible. Even the recently discovered private diaries (*Imo ilgi*:1762) of the court official Yi Kwanghyŏn (1732–?), which render a very anti-Lady Hyegyŏng interpretation of events, are in Chinese, and therefore lose the sense of immediacy that Lady Hyegyŏng's memoirs give. The original record has not survived, but there are fourteen handwritten manuscripts. In Korean literary history, *Hanjung rok* is a canonical court text along with the other celebrated piece, *Naehun*, penned in 1475, by a royal lady, Queen Sohye (1437–1504); and the events narrated in *Hanjung rok* have been continually re-staged in various arenas of Korean popular and high culture.

Why does Crown Prince Sado have such a hold on the Korean imagination? Costume dramas of this period have been continually reproduced since the early days of Korean national television, with various different interpretations but all creeping inevitably to the gruesome climax when the crown prince climbs into the rice-chest, accompanied shortly by the obligatory lightening effects and the collective wailing of the courtiers. Yi In-Wha's novel *Everlasting Empire* (1993)[10] explored and mythologised the court of Chŏngjo. It has since been turned into a hit film starring Korea's national treasure An Sung-ki. This tragic event, commonly referred to as the Imo incident (*Imo hwabyŏn*) of 1762, is much revisited because of its obvious dramatic potential but also because it touches upon so many crucial components of the Korean psyche. Factional identities are still with us, Confucian patrilineal hierarchy, again, is still very much in evidence, and the cautionary morality tale of what happens when one does not live up to one's social and by extension moral obligations that the Imo incident provides, supports the laws of the Confucian moral universe to which many Koreans subscribe. So *Hanjung rok* is a key text in the history not only of Korean literature, but, one could argue, of world literature too, as well as one that has much validity when it comes to interpreting the cultural codes of Korean society today.

However, even though *Hanjung rok* has had tremendous influence on the interpretations of the Imo incident of 1762, it is by no means agreed that Lady Hyegyŏng's version is an objective account. In light of some of the contentious comment *The Red Queen* has received on the grounds that it is not historically accurate, it seems worth while to look into the genesis of the original four memoirs because extra-textual pressures were decisive in shaping the remarkable narratives. Written at four different points in Lady Hyegyŏng's life, each one was prompted by specific incidents and written with definite intent, addressed to concrete narratees, to and for whom she apologises. The compilations in the 19th and early 20th century have edited and organised the volumes in a chronological order which has the effect of erasing the specific reading community to whom they were addressed.

Lady Hyegyŏng wrote the first in 1795, 33 years after the Imo incident. Her son, Chŏngjo, now king, had at the age of eleven witnessed the murder of his father. He, like his grandfather Yŏngjo, was burdened by the question of legitimacy well after his accession to the throne, and had to battle against the opposition of the Pyŏkpa, the party of Principle, led by his step-grandmother, who sought to negate his legitimacy on the grounds of his criminality (by association). He held deeply ambivalent feelings towards his mother and the Hong family and their role in the death of his father. In the first year of his reign, he charged his mother's uncle Hong Inhan with disloyalty and had him executed. The Hongs were besieged. Lady Hyegyŏng wrote the first memoir, in this climate, to her nephew, the heir of the Hong family, as a defence or a justification of the Hongs, in particular the decision to carry on living by herself and with her father after the Imo incident, when it might have seemed more honourable to die.

The second, third and fourth memoirs were written after the death of her son Chŏngjo. Her grandson Sunjo succeeded Chŏngjo but since he was ten years old, it necessitated the regency of Dowager Queen Chŏngsun, Yŏngjo's second queen, and the head of Pyŏkpa, the party of Principle, or the Dogmatist party. Queen

Chŏngsun was a major force is shaping the opposing Pyŏkpa faction against the Hong family's Realist party, Sipa, immediately after the Imo incident; and the Hong family's security was severely threatened again. In 1801, Lady Hyegyŏng's younger brother Hong Nagim was executed, charged of having converted to Catholicism. The second memoir is a posthumous vindication of her brother Hong Nagim and her uncle Hong Inhan and it is written to the child king, her grandson. The third, written in 1802, is also addressed to the boy king, and in it she narrates the dedication of King Chŏngjo, the father of the boy to whom the memoir is addressed, in restoring honour to his own father, Crown Prince Sado. The final memoir was written in 1805 after Sunjo assumed full powers and it finally narrates the Imo incident, focusing on the psychological conflict between father and son and Sado's mental illness, which according to the crown princess was of Caligula-like proportions.

Since her family were heavily involved in the succession disputes, and in the context of when and to whom the memoirs were written, there is no denying that it was in her interests to downplay any political connotations of the Imo incident and to portray it as part of a domestic tragedy. And so Lady Hyegyŏng's narrative has retrospective as well as prospective force. In addition she had to present herself according to prescribed protocols of the court and able to relate only obliquely to questions of legitimate interest. She is a most deeply unreliable narrator. The madness of Crown Prince Sado has been a point of much debate and speculation, but recent revisionist historical accounts approximate him closer to Hamlet than to Caligula. Nevertheless, Lady's Hyegyŏng's account is an undoubted masterpiece, and her control in walking the very thin tightrope of seeming to be neutral while intent on justification is absolute.

The Red Queen is Drabble's literary tribute to *Hanjung rok* in which she absorbs and transforms the original text. *Hanjung rok* is, in turn, a primarily a literary piece of work. And like the preceding memoirs, this fifth memoir also has a specific reading community in mind—the Western reading public[11]. In a curious parallel, the author of this fifth memoir has also become engaged in presentation and preservation of her legacy to the Western reading community; in a similar way, the defensive narrator of *Hanjung rok* was anxious to present and preserve certain legacies.

The novel and its intentions

The starting point for Drabble's variation is a red skirt that Lady Hyegyŏng as child-bride admires. The desire for the beautiful red garment is a common memory that links the author, Drabble and her fictional heroine Babs Halliwell to the crown princess and the colour red is the pigment that runs through the three narratives linking the three personas, giving rise to the title *The Red Queen*, which is a name the crown prince gives to his bride when they are playing 'factional purges' in mock-imitation of the real court situation in which they found themselves.

Organised in three sections, Ancient Times, Modern Times and Postmodern Times, *The Red Queen* first re-tells the story of *Hanjung rok* in first-person narration. But Lady Hyegyŏng's narrative is not merely re-told: it is boldly told from the vantage point of the implied author, Margaret Drabble. Part two jumps to our own times when a modern, successful, independent, middle-aged and very English academic, Dr Halliwell, attends an international conference in Seoul, the journey to which gives her the opportunity to read *Hanjung rok*. If the implied author had been the ghost-narrator of the crown princess's tale in part one, the crown princess/implied author haunts Dr Halliwell in part two. Part three, Postmodern Times, provides the resolution to the preceding narratives with the appearance of the actual author Margaret Drabble herself in the story, who hears about Lady Hyegyŏng from Dr Halliwell and is compelled to re-write the story for the Western audience.

This summary might suggest a linear narrative or a historical reconstruction. But as Drabble insists, this is not an historical novel. In a kind of pre-emptive defence, she writes in the foreword:

> The voice of the Crown Princess, which appears to speak in the first person in the first section of the novel, is not an attempt to reconstruct her real historical voice. It was originally inspired by her voice and her story, but her voice has mixed with mine and with that of Dr Halliwell, and, inevitably, with the voices of her various translators and commentators, all of whom will have brought their own interpretations to her and imposed their personalities upon her. I have not attempted to describe Korean culture or to reconstruct 'real life' in the Korean court of the late eighteenth century.[12]

In spite of her clearly stated intention, some readers have chosen not to take this into account in their interpretations, but to raise a number of questions about representation, appropriation and orientalism. A review in the *Washington Post* of 8 October 2004 is critical of the novel:

> All the orientalist stops are pulled out here...with occasional, jarring, modern asides. I had a lot of trouble...with the modern anachronisms in the first half. I disliked the British self-love that makes England the center of the cultural universe. (Why didn't Lady Hong go off in search of immortality in Ghana or Uzbekistan?)[13]

Similarly, David Jays in *The Observer* (22 August 2004) writes:

> The passing of 200 years can do odd things to a person. In the case of the Crown Princess, she goes a little north London...The author's preface claims that she's searching for 'universal transcultural human characteristics'. The trouble with this quest is that you're likely to run with your own culture, amplifying its ethnics into universality. Drabble

looks at 18th century Seoul and finds Primrose Hill...Trotting in Drabble's wake, reading from her guidebook, the lonely planet just got lonelier.[14]

But the charge that the novel is Anglocentric and anachronistic is curious when Drabble has ostensibly stated from the outset that she will make no attempt at real lifelike mimesis. One could hardly accuse her of failing to reproduce a verisimilitude of the Imo incident when she boldly rejects realist narrative and instead employs a strategy of double temporality in order to pre-empt or at least circumvent the difficulties of cross-cultural interpretations and re-inventions, as picked up by the aforementioned critics. As she writes: "Drawing on a Korean narrative for *The Red Queen* was a foolhardy enterprise, and I was well aware of the dangers, dangers which were an integral part of my theme."[15]

So while *The Red Queen* is in part a variation on the memoirs of Lady Hyegyŏng, the canonical narrative is not repeated as much as relocated to a sphere that is in-between, that wanders about, where everything is hyphenated. Personal identities, cultural identities, and even time are bifurcated, primarily through the method of metempsychosis,[16] and are made formal features of the novel in both theme and structure. This will be discussed in some detail but first a distinction needs to be made between being 'possessed' and being in a state of metempsychosis. Being possessed refers to a soul taking over the mind and body of another being so that there is no internal division between the self and the usurping spirit, which can be a metaphor of colonisation or appropriation. Meanwhile, metempsychosis is a state where one lives through the same experience in the presence of another consciousness which is monitoring, observing, making interpretations of, the other. Being in a state of metempsychosis, is in essence, to be in a state of division or having a hyphenated identity, which in turn could be a metaphor for having a multi-cultural or a transnational-national or a trans-temporal identity.

There are four instances of metempsychosis in the novel: first, the actual author, Margaret Drabble, confesses that she came to write this novel because she was entranced by the memoirs of Lady Hyegyŏng:

> It is sheer chance that the Crown princess came my way at all, but, once I had met her, I could not get her out of my mind. She insisted on my attention. She made me follow her, from text to text, from country to country. She seemed to be making demands on me, but it has not been easy to work out what they might or could be. Several times I have tried to ignore her promptings and to abandon this project, which has been full of difficulties, but she was very persistent.[17]

The second metempsychosis is in part one, Ancient Times, in which Lady Hyegyŏng describes the events of the Imo incident but as how the events might appear were the narrator a product of a late 20th-century Western education. The body might be experiencing the life of a late 18th-century Korean princess, but part of the soul of the narrator has observed and cogitated over the last two hundred years of European intellectual history, philosophy and psychology. Events narrated in *Hanjung rok* are voiced-over with new Western knowledge, and her narration is punctuated by interjections of interpretations from this Western vantage point. For example, she muses that Prince Sado's name recalls the name of the Marquis de Sade. Or again, the ghost princess says: "After much thought, I have come to the conclusion that my husband would now, in your age, be likely to be classified as a paranoid schizophrenic."[18] Posthumously the crown princess has not only acquired the language of psychology and philosophy but she actually conducts research:

> Leafing through an academic periodical the other day, in an attempt to refresh my aged and ageing memory about the composition of the eighteenth-century Chosŏn Court Orchestra, I came by chance across an article by a twentieth-century scholar on the subject of 'Korea and Evil'.[19]

She is so up to the mark in modern academic discourse that she can turn the word himatiophobia in her mind and can dismiss it in favour of the more sensible-sounding clothing phobia. As might be expected, she is conversant with Confucius and Mencius; but also with Sophocles, Voltaire, Freud and Jung. She makes comparative analyses of her experience with those of Napoleon, and Marie Antoinette.

But while it is quite true that Drabble recreates a Lady Hyegyŏng whose identity overtakes the original experiences narrated in *Hanjung rok*, it is equally true that it is not a straightforward imposition. The historical and social identity of Lady Hyegyŏng is conscientiously reconstructed while a psychological identity is radically transported; and the two are continuously aware of, and at times, even construct each other. Tensions between the two selves manifest themselves recurrently throughout part one. At one point the ghost protests:

> I see now that I am beginning to use words that do not belong to me, words that my appointed ghost has whispered in my ear. Postmodern contextualism, enlightenment universalism, deconstruction, concepts of the self. 'Globalization' seems to be one of the words that goes through the restless dreams of my envoy. I do not even know what it means, or what she means by it. Must I try to find out?[20]

And at times, it is not always clear who is speaking and there is a fusion of identities in which both parties mutually constitute one another.

> The relationship between my ghostwriter and myself is uncanny. We are both rationalists, and we both protest that we have no belief in a supernatural life after death. Yet here we are, harnessed together in a ghostly tale of haunting and obsession. We narrate one another, my ghost and I.[21]

The third instance of metempsychosis is in part two when Dr Halliwell is haunted by the amalgam of the implied author and Lady Hyegyŏng:

> The princess is taking her over, bodily and mentally. Dr Babs Halliwell is no longer herself... The princess has entered her, like an alien creature in a science-fiction movie, and she is gestating and growing within her. The pages turn, rapidly, as the princess gains presence and power.[22]

Dr Halliwell, now inhabited by the spirit of the crown princess/ implied author finds many parallels in Seoul. There are many parallels between the cloisters and cabals of Oxford and the Chosŏn court, Halliwell is likened to "a princess of her time".[23] She sees the similarities between the civil and military examination in Chosŏn and modern academic conferences. More importantly she can empathise with the crown princess on a more personal domestic level about irrationality, sickness, violence and infant-deaths, as if space, time and culture posed no barrier.

But this does not give rise to anodyne notions of global cultural unity, for some of the transcultural recognitions are less than universal. The garden of Sŏnggyun'gwan University reminds her overwhelmingly of her paternal grandparents' garden in Orpington.[24] The granite boulders of the Palace Gardens remind her of the artificial landscapes of New York's Central Park.[25] Transcultural recognitions may point to universal characteristics and therefore be unifying; but this section illustrates that they can also be deeply personal, divisive and parochial, offering a sharp critique of Western projections masquerading as unity of cultures.

In the concluding part, we are presented with a natural kind of metempsychosis, through the hyphenated identity of the Chinese baby that Babs Halliwell co-adopts, and whom the spirit of Lady Hyegyŏng sees as a new envoy.

Though the ostensible focus of the novel is Lady Hyegyŏng's life, what Drabble portrays is not necessarily Lady Hyegyŏng's narrative itself but the process of an English mind encountering the other. What is illuminated by the pairing of Chosŏn and postmodern England is not so much Korea or Britain but the cautious and difficult process of a chiasmatic encounter. And more than any sustained plot development, the contrasts provide the central organising principle offering many possibilities to consider 'universality' in the reading of a canonical Korean text. Through four varying degrees of metempsychosis as its device, *The Red Queen* satirises Eurocentrism masquerading as universalism, while at the same time recognising and directly addressing the importance of not simply mimicking a 'nativist' position.

Conclusion

To sum up, *The Red Queen* is both a homage to Lady Hyegyŏng's narrative and a very realistic snapshot of Anglo-Korean relations in the early 21st century because it captures precisely the blurry, in-between, out-of-focus perception of Korea in the British imagination. In her foreword, Drabble states: "...I have asked questions about the nature of survival, and about the possibility of the existence of universal transcultural human characteristics. The Crown Princess was my starting point for this exploration, but not its end."[26] That *The Red Queen* is the starting point for the exploration of Anglo-Korean literary exchange is confirmed by the fact that the translated version of *The Red Queen* into Korean[27] is into its third print, and can be read together with *Hanjung rok* in a wonderful instance of chiasmus. The criss-crossed encounter has given birth to a mutual, reciprocal rebirth of sorts; and the known reversed with the unknown has been transformed by the newly acquired knowledge, resulting in a fusion on the horizon of experience.

Acknowledgement: I would like to thank Dominic Bailey, Angela John, Judith P. Zinsser and Kang Han-rog for discussing, and commenting on, this paper at different stages.

Notes

1. B. S. Johnson, with Michael Bakewell and Giles Gordon (eds), 1975. *You Always Remember the First Time*. London: Quartet Books:166. (Edited and published after Johnson's death in 1973.)
2. Hallyu is, literally translated, 'Korean Wave'. It is a term to denote the explosive reception of Korean popular culture in East Asia. Primarily through the genres of Korean pop music (K-pop), TV dramas and films, Hallyu has had a dramatic impact on the Korean economy. The popularity of Yon Sama, a character in the TV drama *Winter Sonata*, singularly generated an estimated 2 billion *wŏn*s' worth of Korean exports to Japan (see 'Hallyu star power: estimating its value', report of the Korean Parliamentary Research Committee, Seoul, July 2005). Rain is a Korean pop star.
3. Sean Dodson, 2005. 'Whole Lotta Seoul', *The Guardian*, 20 August 2005, Travel section:8.
4. Perry Anderson, 1996. 'Diary', *London Review of Books*, 17 October 1996. See also http://www.changbi.com/english/related/related16.asp, accessed 18 October 2006.
5. Margaret Drabble, 2004. *The Red Queen: A Transcultural Tragicomedy*. London: Viking.
6. The reign of Yŏngjo, the Sage King (1725–76), and that of his grandson Chŏngjo (1776–1800) were the golden years of the latter Chosŏn dynasty. Yŏngjo was the 21st and the longest ruling monarch of Chosŏn, reigning for 51 years, 6 months and 6 days. Great judicious king that he was, Yŏngjo is also famous for his extraordinary 'rice-chest' killing of his son, which has become the stuff of legend in Korean culture.
7. Isabella Bird Bishop, 1897. *Korea and Her Neighbours*. London: John Murray.

8. Drabble, *The Red Queen*:ix.
9. *Sillok*: an official account of each king's reign compiled by the Bureau of State records. The *Chosŏn wangjo sillok* covered the reign of 25 kings from Taejo (1392–98) to Chŏljong (1849–63) in 1,893 volumes.
10. Yin In-Wha, 1993. *Yŏngwonhan chekuk*. Seoul: Segyesa. Translated by Yu Young-Nan as *Everlasting Empire*. New York: Eastbridge, 2002.
11. See Margaret Drabble, 'Only correct', *Times Literary Supplement*, 29 July 2005:12–13.
12. Drabble, *The Red* Queen:ix.
13. Carolyn See, 'Ladies in waiting, past and present', *Washington Post*, 8 October 2004.
14. David Jays, 'Seoul destroying', *The Observer*, 22 August 2004. Online version at http://books.guardian.co.uk/reviews/generalfiction/0,,1288079,00.html, accessed 18 October 2006.
15. Drabble, 'Only correct', *Times Literary Supplement*, 29 July 2005:12.
16. The state of metempsychosis refers to a state where a body is inhabited by another soul which has transmigrated. As a narrative strategy, metempsychosis has had a long history, the most representative and celebrated example being *Ulysses* by James Joyce, where the small-time advertiser and Dubliner, Leopold Bloom, is living the myth of Odysseus.
17. Drabble, *The Red Queen*:vii.
18. ibid.:82.
19. ibid.:83.
20. ibid.:158.
21. ibid.:155.
22. ibid.:184–5.
23. ibid.:173.
24. ibid.:229.
25. ibid.:231.
26. ibid.:x.
27. *Bulgun Wangsaejabin*, trans. Chun Kyung-ja, 2005. Seoul: Munhaksasangsa.

THE EVOLUTION OF MUSEUMS IN THE REPUBLIC OF KOREA

KEITH PRATT

For all that the Chosŏn *yangban* took such pride in their sinocentric culture, they could not claim to have kept up with their Chinese neighbours in the tradition of connoisseurship. Put bluntly, the majority of them simply had not cultivated the habit of collecting bronzes, porcelain, and the paintings of bygone ages, or commissioning new works of art, with the enthusiasm and expertise that great Chinese households had. There were exceptions of course: Prince Anpyŏng (1418–53) owned Chinese paintings from the Tang to Yuan periods, including no less than sixteen by Guo Xi (*c*.1020–*c*.1090), and he patronised the artist An Kyŏn (1400–?), whose still extant and well-known *Dream Journey to Peach Blossom Spring* reveals the influence Guo (and/or his patron the prince) had on him. But it may be that the Imjin Wars of the last decade of the 16th century, besides annihilating collections such as the prince's, also helped undermine the gentry's disposition to invest in destructible goods through the 17th and 18th centuries. The royal family itself, however, could hardly fail to follow the acquisitive example set by the great Ming and Qing emperors, especially during the long and generally settled reigns of Yŏngjo and Chŏngjo, so it is not surprising that the first museum in Korea should be that attached to the imperial household. Its opening in Changgyŏng palace in 1909, during the threatening days of the Japanese protectorate (1905–10), was doubtless intended to make a positive statement about the nature and quality of Korea's own culture, albeit with tacit admission of its indebtedness to China, but following annexation in 1910, the institution was re-branded (1915) as the Chōsen Sōtokufu Museum and then, instead of Korean independence, the priority was to demonstrate the integrity of Korean and Japanese civilisation.

Whatever one may think of the motives for the extensive archaeological work undertaken by the Japanese in Manchuria and northern Korea during the colonial period, neither the importance of their many discoveries nor the academic quality of their published reports is in doubt. Historic Sites Preservation Societies were established in Kyŏngju and Puyŏ; the repair and restoration of many historic

Fig.1. The Japanese Government-General Building, later the National Museum of Korea (photo by courtesy of the Korea Overseas Information Service—KOIS)

monuments and buildings was begun after centuries of neglect; and provincial museums were established in Kaesŏng (1931), Pyŏngyang (1932) and Kongju (1940). But wealthy Korean patriots were also laying the groundwork for museum collections of the future. They included Chŏn Hyŏngpil, founder of today's Kansong Museum, and Kim Sŏngsu, who helped turn round the struggling Posŏng College and form what later became Koryŏ University Museum. It is now one of the country's foremost museums with important collections of paintings and sculpture.

In the aftermath of the Japanese occupation, politicians recognised the need to remind people of what Korea had once been and what it must struggle to become again. In 1945 the Chōsen Sōtokufu Museum re-opened its doors to the public, but now it was named the National Museum of Korea (NMK) and its doors were in the Capitol Building, the former Government-General headquarters; university museums like those of Ewha and Seoul National (formerly Keijō Imperial University) were re-established; and 1946 saw the foundation of the National Folk Museum (NFM) and Inchŏn City Museum. But then the Korean War brought fresh crisis. The NFM was destroyed, but it is claimed that the evacuation of the National Museum to Pusan saved nearly 75 per cent of its 27,000 pieces. Three years later, the rival regimes in north and south began the competition to establish their credibility as defenders of pan-Korean culture. North Korea opened the Central Historical Museum in Pyŏngyang.

South of the Demilitarised Zone, the NMK returned to Seoul, first to temporary premises on Namsan, then to a more settled home in Tŏksugung. The National Folk Museum took longer to re-establish, and did not re-open until 1966. Three years after that, in 1969, the National Museum for Contemporary Art (NMCA) opened in Kyŏngbokgung premises. This was a new and important institution, representing an unprecedented outreach towards the wider international art community and a follow-up to the artist Park Seo-bo's appearance at the Paris Biennale in 1961.[1] But commitment to art proved a costly exercise, and within three years pressure on space meant that the major museums were on the move once more. In 1972, the National Museum of Korea took possession of a new building in Kyŏngbokgung, a splendid headquarters surmounted with a yellow-tiled pagoda; the following year, NMCA removed to Sŏkjojŏn in Tŏksugung, and in 1975, the National Folk Museum also relocated, into a building of its own in Kyŏngbokgung.

Throughout the Park Chung Hee era (1961–79), the government invested heavily in new museums. Around 76 were opened, including new branches of the National Museum in Kyŏngju, Kongju and Puyŏ that were built to imaginative architectural designs reflecting regional tradition and style.[2] A feature of this period was the proliferation of university museums. The art historian Kim Won-young told me in 1978 that the reason there were so many was that the government had required all universities to establish a museum. This had stimulated their departments of archaeology to unearth objects to put in them, while at the same time helping to foster pride in the nation's past—which was exactly the government's intention. Some were little more than a single room and enjoyed only a short life, but others grew into large and well-respected institutions which now hold particularly strong collections. Donga University Museum in Pusan, for example, established in 1959, has 25,000 artefacts dating from Neolithic to Chosŏn times, and is especially strong on the early history of the southeast region of the peninsula. Other university museums were lucky enough to attract donations from private collectors, an example which continues to be followed to the present. One of these was Dankook University, where the museum founded in 1967 acquired the comprehensive collection of Chosŏn-period costumes now displayed in its Suk Joosun Memorial Museum (established in 1981); another was Kyung Hee University, which opened the Hye Jung Museum for the 150 old maps donated by Kim Hye-jung in 2005. Besides the emphasis on museums, the government initiated other measures to shore up traditional culture and prevent it from slipping into obscurity and oblivion. The Cultural Properties Protection Law (1962) introduced the system of classifying Tangible and Intangible Cultural Assets, a scheme which Keith Howard has investigated in detail.[3] Ten years later, in 1972, the Culture and Arts Promotion Law was introduced, leading to the establishment of the Korea Culture and Arts Foundation and the Culture and Arts Promotion Fund. But government funding went almost entirely into officially approved projects, and "artists and art groups out of line with official cultural policy found it difficult, even impossible, to get public support".[4] Minjung arts were not recognised, and when I visited the National Folk Museum in 1974 neither its contents nor their display impressed me, though when the Folk Village opened near Suwŏn that year it did pay further lip service of a kind to the role of the peasantry in traditional society. (When I re-visited the Village thirty years on, however, I was struck by how much more attention was then being paid to the social customs, arts and work skills of the lower classes. By that time, too, the National Folk Museum had been transformed into a large, excellent collection with imaginatively filled rooms intent on teaching and enthusing the public, especially including children, with the story of the Korean people's characteristics and qualities during their rapid transition from tradition to modernity.)

One man who was never afraid to proclaim the quality of Korean folk art, well before it began to take its proper place alongside literati art as a subject for aesthetic admiration, was Zo Zayong (Cho Cha-yong; 1926–2000). In 1968 he founded his Emille Museum, which would soon establish a reputation as a foremost protector and showcase of native Korean arts, and despite being out of favour with the military regime he became the first president of the Korean Museum Association (KMA) when it was founded in 1974.

Through the 1980s, anxiety about the watering down of traditional culture at home prompted an increase in major capital projects. In view of the approaching Seoul Olympics (1988), nationalistic and self-aggrandising purposes underlay many of these: 1984, for example, saw the initiation of Seoul Arts Center, 1985 the decision to found the Seoul City Museum (completed in 1997 and opened in 2002 as the Seoul Museum of History), 1986 the opening of a new building for the National Museum for Contemporary Art at Kwachŏn and that of a second Folk Village, this time in Kyŏngju. In that same year, the National Museum of Korea moved across the Kyŏngbokgung compound and into the Capitol Building (vacating its old building for eventual occupation by the NFM). All this cost money. The share of the total central government budget allocated to culture rose from 0.17 per cent in 1981 to 1.04 per cent in 1995. Local government gave 1.7 per cent of its budget to culture in 1987, rising to 2.1 per cent in 1995.[5] Of this, a considerable portion went into buildings rather than activities. Concern was also expressed at the quantity of Korean relics held in museums abroad, and in 1986 the International Cultural Society of Korea, forerunner of the Korea Foundation, embarked on an ambitious project to document them. Beginning in 1989, a series of lavish volumes catalogued the major holdings of Korean artefacts at museums in the United States, Western Europe, and Japan.

All these were developments of major national import and more were to follow. In 1992, the National Palace Museum was established in Tŏksugung, and in 1994 the National War Memorial was opened in Yongsan. This excellent museum documents the history of warfare across the Korean peninsula from Neolithic times to the present, as well as providing the public with its principal visual resource for the 1950–53 war. Also in 1995, the demolition of the Capitol Building signalled the beginning of a long-term project for the archaeological study of Kyŏngbok palace and the reconstruction of many of the buildings within it that had been destroyed by the Japanese from 1910 onwards. It was acknowledgement of what Choi Sungja, of *Hanguk Ilbo*, had written in 1993: "The younger generation...have matured fully understanding the old traditions. Hence, the preservation of our traditional culture must be undertaken seriously for posterity. The best way for Korea to contribute to world culture is for it first to develop its own traditional culture...An active movement is growing among young people today to study it and understand it."[6] Taking a Seoul-centric view, he claimed that most of the NMK regional branches were inaccessible to the public, and said that "many of their cultural treasures are displayed without sufficient explanation of their significance...On the other hand, specialized museums, which collect and display relics that were used by the people until quite recently, exude a warm, nostalgic atmosphere."

Certainly, the 1990s might almost be designated the decade of the specialist museum. Under the direction of Lee O-young as first holder in 1990 of the newly created post of Minister of Culture, state control over culture was relaxed, and with the devolution and democratisation of cultural policies an array of new museums began to appear. Some were private or corporate foundations (e.g. the Hyundae Gallery); some run by local authorities (e.g. the Kyŏnggi Provincial Museum); others attached to universities. Some spread their net wide, others concerned themselves with individual countries, e.g. the World Jewellery Museum, the Pan-Asian Paper Museum, the Tibet Museum. Some were Korea-specific, e.g. the Kimchi Museum, the Korean Christian Museum, the Korean Shamanism Museum; and some were confined to local history, such as the Tongdosa Temple Museum and the Mirŭksa Temple Museum. Some were general in coverage, such as the Horim Museum in Seoul, established by Yun Chang-sop in 1982, which opened a new building in 1999. Its current collection boasts pottery, porcelain, paintings, books, and metalwork, including eight National Treasures. Others were specific as to their content (e.g. the Hahoe Mask Museum). Some were devoted to individuals, for example, the Ojukheon Museum in Kangnŭng, commemorating the great philosopher Yi I (brush-name Yulgok; 1536–84), and the Whanki Museum, Seoul, honouring the painter Kim Whanki (brush-name Suhwa; 1913–74), or were connected with living individuals, e.g. the wood sculpture and Buddhist artefacts collection associated with the craftsman Mok-A. Some, such as a Straw and Plants Handicrafts Museum, reflected the minjung movement's revelation that art and aestheticism were to be found even in the day-to-day activities of the working classes; Seoul's Artsonje Art Museum, on the other hand, was holistic in a different way, linking museology and the environment.[7]

Following the establishment of the Korean Business Council for the Arts in 1994, commercial sponsorship—albeit fluctuating, especially during 1997–8—increased. Shortly before the economic crisis hit, 1997 had been designated the Year of Cultural Heritage. Publicity was given to the need to rescue treasures from being destroyed or reburied by building projects and to protect Korean culture against imported global features; and emphasis was given to raising public awareness of and reviving traditional customs, and to restoring ancient buildings. The government had caught on to the realisation that museums (along with other cultural forms and events) promote tourism, and that tourism strengthens the economy.[8] Nor was it oblivious to the fact that museums help to promote nationalism. Whilst, ironically, today's NMK website complains that the Japanese Government-General "utilized" the museums established in Kaesŏng and Pyŏngyang in 1931 and 1932 "as a political instrument rather than a disinterested means to display Korean culture", the government of the Republic of Korea (ROK) itself nevertheless launched:

- The Diplomatic History Museum in Seoul, in 1993, displaying interesting materials from 1887 onwards, but later brought up to date with exhibitions on the Tokto and Koguryŏ disputes with Japan and China
- The National War Memorial in Seoul, in 1994, where nationalistic themes are only to be expected, but where the role of the United Nations forces, even those of the United States, in the Korean War passes almost unnoticed in the indoor rooms. (The open-air assemblage of aircraft, tanks and weaponry, however, cannot conceal the ROK's heavy dependence on American aid.)
- The Tokto Museum on Ullŭngdo, in 1997

In July–August 2005, the Korea International Exhibition Center at Koyang in Kyŏnggi province hosted the 2005 World Museum Culture Expo. Showing items from 22 countries, including loans from the Hermitage, Louvre, and Taipei National Palace Museums, this was—despite its title—primarily a Korean venture, designed, in the words of Jung Yu-ran, author of a *Pictorial Korea* article (8/2005), "to promote awareness of and pride in Korea's cultural and historical legacies…The exposition also aims to strengthen Korea's international competitiveness by…developing…tourism resources, *and dispute false claims made by neighbouring countries regarding Korean history and culture*" (my italics).[9] None of these might exactly be called disinterested means of displaying Korean culture.

The museum-founding trend continued into the 21st century. In the 18 to 24 months of 2004–05, *Pictorial Korea* ran articles on specific museums, almost all of them new establishments. Among the newcomers were an Aerospace Museum, a European Porcelain Museum, a Gugak Record Museum, and a Chocolate Museum. The educational role of museums was taken on board and many dedicated special areas or exhibitions of interest to children; though in others, e.g. a Kitchen Utensils Museum and a Beer Museum, it must be admitted, children's interests were likely to take a fairly definite second place to those of their parents. In a sense, of course, all museums are educational, and offer plentiful opportunities for ideological or political messages to be driven home. Hence in February to March 2005, ironically the year dedicated in advance to Korean-Japanese friendship, the Samsung Museum of Publishing ran a special exhibition of books, journals and music banned during the colonial era, ranging from obvious candidates such as those on socialism or Admiral Yi Sunsin to Cheong Jiyong's poetry collection *Baekrokdam* ('White Deer Pool').[10] The exhibition coincided with street demonstrations in Seoul against Japan's claim to the Tokto islands.

According to the Korean National Commission for UNESCO (KNCU),[11] South Korea had 174 museums in 1996. Of these, 23 were major national museums covering history, arts, science, folk art, post, railways, etc. and came under the direct responsibility of the central government; 24 were public museums, 47 private museums and 80 university museums. In addition, KNCU counted 32 art museums (one national, four public and 27 private). There were also 269 exhibition venues and 337 private galleries throughout the country. The 1999 *Handbook of Korea* (published by the Korea Overseas Information Service) referred to 12 National Museums, "about 33" local museums (including municipal ones), 81 university museums, 88 private ones, 42 "specialty museums" (devoted, *inter alia*, to business, textbooks, communications, and military history), and 33 art museums: total 277. In contrast, the website for the Ministry of Culture and Tourism, uploaded in 2001 and still not updated in summer 2006, says there are 233 museums in Korea. A paper given to the 2004 meeting in Seoul of the International Committee for Architecture and Museum Techniques (ICAMT) referred to a total of 260 museums (41 public, 162 private, 57 university), or 1:190,000 per head of population.[12] These figures are at best vague and sometimes contradictory: I suspect they were already an underestimate when they were published, and are certainly so now. The 2005 website of the Korean Museums Association (KMA), which should be authoritative, speaks of over five hundred museums across Korea,[13] and the 2006 website of the University Museums and Collections (UMAC) Database counts 89 representatives in South Korea.[14] The count grows with regularity, some of the newcomers being the lifetime obsessions of private collectors who present their own collections to public scrutiny, like Choi Hongkyu, who opened his Lock Museum in 2003, showing examples of locks and latches from the Silla to Chosŏn periods, or Kim Dong-hui, whose Oil Lamp Museum is one of the several varied private museums to be visited at Yongin in Kyŏnggi province. This trend has been encouraged since 2004 by the possibility of subsidy from the KMA's allocation of the government's lottery revenue.[15] The number and scope of so many foundations, large and small, really stretch the imagination, all the more if one extends the list to include art galleries, the most important of which, such as the Samsung and Hyundae Galleries in Seoul, regularly mount major exhibitions that put them on a par with permanent museum displays. A huge number of galleries have sprouted, not only around Insa-dong in Seoul but in cities and towns across the country. There were 527 of them in 1999, according to KOIS, another figure that is again likely to be an underestimate by now. And then there are the outdoor 'museums', including shrines such as that to Yi Sunsin at Asan, folk villages, sculpture parks, theme parks (including the destroyer that can be toured at the Sapgyoho Marine Park in Dangjin in South Chungchŏng province), and archaeological sites such as Amsadong Neolithic park in Seoul.

In 1993, Oh Kwang-su wrote that: "An art museum is a vessel for art. The building gives shape to the works of art inside the museum."[16] And, I would add, vice versa. Two recent museums, both private foundations, show how buildings and their contents can complement each other perfectly. In the modest building of the Whanki Museum (1992), the Korean-American architect Kyu Sung Woo combines the spirit of tradition and modernity, and the feeling for *pungsu*—respect for its setting— with the forms favoured by Korea's leading abstract artist Kim Whanki. It is an innovative and sensitive construction, a building that fits into its background on Pugak mountain as country homesteads once nestled into folds in the hills, both complementing and

Fig.2. The Whanki Museum, Seoul (photo: K. L. Pratt)

enhancing the famous works of art it contains: a combination of *yin* and *yang*, the natural and the artificial, the curved and the straight, the abstract and the physical. Two rounded tops to an end wall evoke the shoulders of the *meibyŏng* vase, the epitome to Kim of his country's cultural heritage and a shape that was central to the art of his early period. Beneath the eaves a line of small windows, and below them a design of light and dark tiles, anticipate the patterns he created in the early 1970s as he explored the possibilities of dots and squares. Inside is a cool combination of light, space, and proportion. Staircases, galleries, and showrooms rise around a central atrium, making skilful use of natural light shining through effectively placed openings. Space has been carefully planned, walls made appropriate for large and small works, and floors for free-standing showcases displaying papier-mâché creations from the late 1960s and early 1970s.

In 2005, the Samsung Foundation, already a major arts sponsor through the Hoam Museum and its downtown gallery in Soonhwa-dong in Seoul, opened its Leeum Museum in Yongsan. It is actually two museums, one devoted to traditional Korean arts, the other to Korean and Western modern and contemporary art. Designed by different architects—Mario Botta and Jean Nouvel respectively—and with a third element, the Samsung Child Education and Culture Center, by Rem Koolhaas, the entire complex is a perfect illustration of Oh Kwang-su's observation. (In passing, Museum 1 is claimed to evoke the shape of an ancient Korean fortress, something also claimed for Kyŏnggi Provincial Museum, the walls of which replicate those of the nearby Hwasŏng castle, the NMCA, *and* the new NMK. Fortresses may afford reassurance as to the security of the treasures they house, but are not known for being aesthetically innovative or exciting, and this preoccupation with military defensiveness, while underlining Korea's great historical traditions, also hints at continuing political unease at the expense of architectural innovation.) In Museum 1 of the Leeum Museum, the use of softly coloured materials, curved walls, sympathetic lighting, and small cases and generous spacing mean that building and treasures wrap around and nestle comfortably into each other. In Museum 2, where straight lines, right angles and wider open spaces are the rule and the internal division into interconnecting exhibition 'boxes' devoted to individual artists corresponds appropriately with the rectangular frames hanging on the walls, the quantity of glass and stainless steel contributes to a more modern atmosphere, yet one that still brings visitors into close visual contact with the surrounding hillside and trees through wide window areas, and reminds them of the natural world as the source of building materials. The theme is taken up by many of the exhibits, especially the installation works, illustrating how much can be done with wood, metal, wool, clay, etc.

One can learn a lot about the values and priorities of a country and its people from its museums. During visits to Korea over the past 34 years, I have seen many of them, and have witnessed not just their numerical growth and a widening of their subject range, but also an evolution in their underlying purposes (the expression of ideology and the shaping of educational aims) and their physical attributes (especially their architecture and display methods). I was in Korea when the National Museum of Korea opened its new home in the Kyŏngbok palace in 1972 (as I was again, incidentally, in 1974 when the #1 line of the Seoul subway was opened. Given the major part played by Japanese companies in the construction of the line, the date chosen for the ceremony—15 August, Liberation Day—did not go unremarked). I was not in Korea on 15 August 1987, when the Independence Hall opened in Chŏnan, "dedicated to the history of the Korean people's struggles against foreign invaders...a sacred place that symbolizes the people's triumph over national crisis." Nor again in 1995 when the demolition of the old Japanese Government-General headquarters—the Capitol Building—began, also on 15 August. Roh Tae Woo had approved this symbolic act in 1990. Its appeal to Korean patriots was easy to see, but it provoked strong objections from some Koreans to whom it acted as a necessary reminder of the past, and from foreigners who appreciated it as one of the finest examples of 20th-century architecture in East Asia. In 1995 it was in use as the home of the National Museum, and a corollary of Kim Young Sam's decision to implement his predecessor's decision was the need to find land and money for a suitable replacement.

Fig.3. The National Museum of Korea, Yongsan, Seoul (photo: KOIS)

Fig.4. National Museum of Korea: 'castle effect' (photo: K. L. Pratt)

Fig.5. National Museum of Korea: Kyŏngchŏnsa pagoda (photo: K. L. Pratt)

Grandiose plans were aired and almost immediately put in jeopardy by the economic crisis of 1997–8, but on 28 October 2005 there I was again, this time to witness the opening of a new National Museum, the completion of its seventh move. It was what Barry Lord, a ICAMT Board member, speaking at the ICAMT meeting in Seoul the previous year, had called "one of the most important examples of the reassertion of national identities [sic]...as you have torn down a museum building that was a symbol of oppression and replaced it with a new national museum."[17] As another commentator, Yani Herreman, vice-president of the International Council of Museums, put it: "Identity is a contemporary issue that has become undeniable in museum practice."[18]

The new National Museum of Korea deserves to be trumpeted around the world for its buildings, its contents, and the confidence of successive governments in pushing ahead with the project against political and economic odds.[19] Its chosen location constituted one of the very first problems. It was at Yongsan, near the north bank of the Han river in Seoul, which despite its ideal *pungsu* was also the headquarters of the US Army in the ROK. For a long time this had been almost as great an irritant to Korean nationalists as the old Capitol Building had been and they would be delighted to see it go. The US authorities eventually agreed to move out, and though construction began in 1997, the opening of the Museum was two years later than scheduled, partly because of delays in resiting the American helipad. In 1999, one estimate of the total cost of the operation had amounted to US$246m,[20] and the final count, excluding the initial land purchase, is said to have been around US$400 million.[21] The international design competition was won by Kim Jangil, whose creation was intended to represent a "safe and peaceful fortress" between Mount Namsan and the artificial lake dug in the grounds in front of the museum. If his vision for what would become in terms of acreage the world's sixth biggest museum missed out on a chance to create a monument to Korean powers of architectural innovation, one cannot fail to be impressed by the way Mr Kim's own understanding of lightness and proportion matches the lightness of touch and sense of scale which belonged to so many of the ancient craftsmen represented in its display rooms.[22] Even the newly restored, ten-storey marble pagoda from Kyŏngchŏnsa standing at one end of the main gallery neither dominates nor is diminished by its surroundings. Eleven thousand of the estimated 150,000 items in the Museum's collection were on display for the opening, and rooms on the third floor displayed treasures from neighbouring countries and related cultures, thus helping to illustrate Korea's position in the spread of world civilisation.

The new museum represents the unique cultural features and standards that have always attracted me to Korea. I was among those who lamented the decision to demolish the National Museum's previous accommodation, and I still mourn the loss of such a splendid building, but I welcome the value placed on the past, present and future that its successor, and the burgeoning number of other new museums across the ROK, represent. And whilst I recognise the essential relationship between museum collections and an affirmation of national identity, I also welcome the element of internationalism that characterises the best of Korea's new museums, both in their design and display philosophy.[23]

Notes

1. Koreans had exhibited paintings in Japan during the colonial period and begun to work in France after Liberation, but this was the first Western exhibition of significance by a contemporary Korean artist.
2. According to Professor Lim Sang-Oh, these replaced six regional outposts of the Syngman Rhee era that had been identical in design and size and had each been given the same financial resources, and had thus proved unable to measure up to their quite different requirements (interview, 12 November 2003).
3. Keith Howard, 1990. 'The tangible and intangible Korean heritage: protection, preservation, and presentation', *Che 3-ch'a Chosonhak kukche haksul t'oronhoe, nonmun yoji*. Osaka: Osaka kyongje popkwa taehak:425–6. Critics have claimed that Park's interest was not so much in saving Korean culture for its own sake, but in exploiting it to strengthen his own

fledgling political legitimacy and to tap its economic potential. See Lim Sang-Oh, 2002. 'Support policy of culture in a comparative view: some lessons from Korean experience'. Paper prepared for the 12th International Conference on Cultural Economics, Rotterdam, June 2002:9. [Unpublished]

4. Lim, 2002: ibid.:12.
5. Lim Sang-Oh, 2001. 'Cultural economics and cultural policy in Korea'. *Korean Journal of Cultural Economics* 4/Pt. 2:130.
6. *Koreana* 7/4, 1993:78.
7. "The neighboring areas of Artsonje, reborn as a new and experimental avenue, create a harmonious combination together with the elegant, geometric structures of Artsonje's buildings. Located at the historical and traditional area of Samchong-dong surrounded by old palaces and traditional houses, Artsonje has contributed in making the area the new, cultural hub with its involvement in the most up-to-date, contemporary art culture." http://www.artsonje.org, accessed 1 October 2006.
8. By 2000, however, it had identified another priority, also with attractive economic prospects, and most of its cultural budget had been diverted away from arts institutions and into events and industries, especially film and IT-related entertainment enterprises.
9. *Pictorial Korea* 8/2005:29.
10. Cheong's work continued to be barred in the ROK itself until 1988.
11. http://www.culturelink.or.kr/policy_korea.html, accessed 1 October 2006.
12. cf. Japan 1:42,000, USA 1:60,000, Germany 1:20,000. In the UK there were reckoned to be ±2,500 museums and galleries at the end of 2005.
13. http://www.museum.or.kr/english/index.htm, accessed 1 October 2006. KMA was established in 1976.
14. http://publicus.culture.hu-berlin.de/collections/list.php?id=i&l=South+Korea.
15. Ariane Perrin, 2005. 'Private museums in Korea'. *Asian Art*, December 2005:8.
16. *Koreana* 7/4, 1993:80.
17. Barry Lord: see http://www.culture.gr/2/21/215/21506/Brief25.doc, accessed 1 October 2006.
18. See ibid.
19. Chung, Yun Shun Susie, 2003. 'Object as exhibit: legitimising the building of the National Museum of Korea'. *International Journal of Heritage Studies* 9/3:229–42.
20. M. S. Kang, 1999. 'Kyongbok Palace: history, controversy, geomancy'. *Manoa* 11/2:5.
21. http://weekly.hankooki.com/lpage/culture/200510/wk2005102519060837140.htm, accessed 1 October 2006.
22. Keith Pratt, 2006. 'National Museum of Korea reopens'. *Asian Art*, January 2006:422.
23. Many of these museums have excellent websites, often in English, Japanese and Chinese as well as Korean.

THE WORLD KOREANISTS FORUM 2005 AND KOREAN STUDIES

Don Starr

The invitation to the World Koreanists Forum 2005,[1] described as being "For the Global Network of Korean Studies", came as the result of a response[2] I had sent to the web-based Korean Studies Discussion List on the problems facing Korean studies departments in the United Kingdom. (All such departments are, in fact, located in English universities, but serve the whole of the UK.) The theme of the Forum was at least in part a reaction to a letter by Dr Jay Lewis on the plight of Korean studies at Oxford, which had appeared earlier in the year in the *Chosun Ilbo*. My brief was to give a paper under the title: 'The crisis of Korean studies in the UK: causes and countermeasures'.[3]

The conference seems to have been a rather last-minute affair (workers were still re-laying the roads when we arrived), aimed in part at launching a revamped Academy for Korean Studies (AKS), which was absorbing the old Korea Research Foundation. Two things in the background were Dr Lewis's article in the *Chosun Ilbo*, which was being used by supporters of Korean studies in Korea to try to persuade the government to increase its funding of Korean studies, and a more domestic concern by the AKS to show it was taking seriously its enhanced role as a torch-bearer for the subject. The *Chosun Ilbo* report, which appeared on 29 March 2005, specifically linked the issue of Korean studies abroad with Korea's strategic interests. It referred to the Tokto islets issue and complained that the more generous funding of Japanese studies by the Japanese government was helping promote an international view of the dispute that was favourable to Japan.[4] The following day an editorial comment followed up this report, contrasting Korean studies support unfavourably with Japan's expenditure on promoting Japanese studies programmes overseas, which it claimed amounted to US$500 million a year, or 100 times Korea's 5.4 billion *wŏn* (US$5.4 million).[5] The editorial asked: "How can we stop anyone from describing the East Sea as the 'Sea of Japan' in these circumstances, or from mislabelling the Dokdo Islets, which are undoubtedly Korean, as Takeshima."[6] The *Chosun Ilbo* had also asked the previous day whether the Korean government's announcement that it was strengthening Korean studies through the Academy of Korean Studies was only hot air. The pressure was on the AKS to do something, and the World Koreanists Forum 2005 was the result. It began at the AKS's impressive site on the outskirts of Seoul with an opening ceremony that led with a keynote speech by Vice-Prime Minister Kim Jin Pyo. He was followed by the president of AKS, Yoon Deok Hong and other notables, all with simultaneous interpretation and a host of reporters.

The Forum was organised around four regional groups: China and Japan, Oceania and Southeast Asia, North and South America, and Europe and the Middle East, with a total of 28 papers on aspects of Korean studies. It was clear that there were big differences in the state of Korean studies in the different countries represented, but these boiled down to either supply side or demand side issues, or both. The countries suffering most tended to be those with relatively low levels of Korean support and low levels of student demand, especially where the national funding model was closely linked to student demand. In those doing best, support and demand were both present. For example, Thailand has one of the most extensive programmes, with 16 universities or campuses offering Korean studies; it relies to a considerable extent on support from the Korea International Cooperation Agency (KOICA), an organisation not active in developed countries.[7] In the United States, the immigrant Korean community supports Korean studies by enrolling on Korean studies courses in large numbers and offering direct financial support. In other countries, for example, in the UK, no significant Korean community exists, or it may exist but does not offer the same support, as in Australia, for example. Participants in the Forum focussed on their particular deficiencies: lack of funds, lack of other resources or lack of students. Some objected to the use of the word 'crisis' in my presentation, on the grounds that this was overstating the problems in the UK. My response to this was, firstly, that I was writing to the title supplied by the Academy for Korean Studies and, secondly, that while some UK departments teaching Korean, such as at the School for Oriental and African Studies (SOAS), were flourishing, others including Durham (my own) and Newcastle were being closed, while others still, such as Oxford, were at that time under threat. This certainly felt like a crisis to at least some of those involved.

Background to the UK's problems

A direct cause of this crisis was a change in the UK funding system in 1998–9, which took away protection from subjects by breaking the link between the quota of students studying a particular subject and the pot of cash dedicated to supporting that activity. This was presented as a move from a planned economy to a market-led one. Against a background of funding cuts in real terms throughout the 1990s,[8] vice-chancellors of English universities sought, and won, agreement from the government funding body, the Higher Education Funding Council for England (HEFCE), for a more entrepreneurial, market-led approach. Universities would continue to receive their historic tuition funding levels provided they maintained absolute student numbers and did not make drastic changes to the subject mix. To cope with real-terms funding cuts, universities introduced tighter budgetary control, with many devolving budgets to departments. These were based on a department's actual student enrolment at the rates paid by HEFCE, in spite of the fact that HEFCE has always insisted its fee bands are 'broad brush' and should be adjusted at local level according to need and actual costs. The mixed message that this gave, on the one hand asking universities to function like commercial businesses in pursuit of maximum profit and on the other calling for cross-subsidisation, allowed senior managements wide scope for personal discretion in what they chose to support or abandon.

These changes allowed universities to close down subjects or departments without this having an impact on the historic tuition income figures, provided overall student numbers were maintained. Less popular or higher-cost subjects could be dropped, with the quota switched into lower-cost or more popular subjects. This led to a flurry of chemistry department closures, ostensibly as a result of low demand. Demand was defined in consumer terms, as applicants for the subject, rather than national or employer demand for graduate chemists. Only in the case of medicine was there still a planned approach, attempting to match the output of graduates to national demand.

Where Korean was taught as a full honours subject, i.e. at SOAS and Sheffield University, it continued to be eligible for additional HEFCE minority funding, and so was not affected at this point.[9] This system did not include departments teaching Korean courses making up less than 50 per cent of a student's time, as at Oxford, Cambridge, Durham and Newcastle, which received no earmarked funding for teaching the subject. However, in 2005, following a HEFCE report[10] into the minority funding system, it was decided to incorporate the minority subject funding into the block grants of the universities concerned, also removing this protection from major courses in Korean.

A further problem for intensively taught subjects, such as languages, has been the impact of the Research Assessment Exercise (RAE).[11] Unlike excellence in teaching, excellence in research as measured by the RAE brings substantial amounts of extra cash, in addition to great kudos. This has encouraged universities to focus increasingly on research, leading to a reduction in staff teaching hours and student contact hours, and favouring less intensively taught, 'library-based' subjects where staff can devote more time to research. Conversely, it has disadvantaged intensive teaching subjects, especially those where an external measure of teaching effectiveness exists and where a department has to bear the financial and research burden of funding non-research-active staff, such as language instructors. Each research-active member of staff can, in principle, bring in additional funding of over £30,000 per year for the duration of the RAE period in question.[12] Hence a library-based subject such as history, not requiring intensive teaching, may attract a supplement of £30,000 per year for every member of staff in the department, whereas a 'hard' language is likely to have up to 40 per cent of staff as language instructors attracting no supplementary payments. The extra teaching burden also impacts on the research productivity of research-active staff.[13]

Making the case for Korean studies in the UK

Although lip-service is paid to the importance of language learning in the UK,[14] in practice it tends to be regarded as a skill rather than an academic subject. This has become much more pronounced as the RAE system has redefined the standard of success for a department. A former chief executive of HEFCE was reported as saying he believed that language teaching was not an appropriate university subject and should be taught in language schools, not in universities.[15] My own vice-chancellor (a medical man), in discussing his decision to close down the Department of East Asian Studies at Durham, told me that the subject was like nursing: it lacked disciplinary methodology and would never make the grade in research. Since two of the seven departments of East Asian studies gained the highest 5* research grade in the 2001 RAE, and none fell below a grade 4, this was somewhat wide of the mark.[16] However, he was reflecting a widespread view of modern language teaching,[17] which has fallen into a language centre limbo of low-level language-only courses in many universities. Traditionally, modern European languages have been taught in language and literature departments, while East Asian studies has tended to be taught in a broader area-studies environment, one which resembles more the teaching of classics in the UK.[18]

However, campaigns against the closure of East Asian language courses have had an effect. The ambassadors of Japan and Korea have made representations to the British Foreign and Commonwealth Office and HEFCE, and the chambers of commerce have also lobbied. One result of this was the then Minister of Education, Charles Clarke, ordered an enquiry into the state of strategic and vulnerable subjects in UK universities in December 2004. This resulted in a HEFCE report in June 2005 that identified certain area studies and related minority languages as strategic *and* vulnerable; one of the three groups identified was "Japanese, Chinese, Mandarin [*sic*] and other far eastern languages and area studies."[19] We can assume that Korean is included in this group, although it is not specifically named. HEFCE's general position has been that there is little demand from employers for speakers of East Asian languages and there is no national need for a significant corpus of graduates with higher-level language skills (CEF level C1 & C2, Language Ladder 13–14).[20] Based on its own sources, the HEFCE view has been that British companies will prefer to hire native speakers of the language concerned, and any expatriates will require only survival language skills. However, in an important shift at this time, pressed by the area studies associations[21] among others, HEFCE conceded that discipline-based researchers working on East Asia needed to acquire sufficient linguistic skill to be able to read original sources and participate in academic debates with colleagues in East Asia. It was no longer appropriate to support researchers working solely from English or other European languages for most East Asia-centred research topics. The initiative HEFCE announced was intended to remedy this specific perceived academic need, not to support undergraduate language study, which was already subvented by HEFCE's regular funding regime.[22]

Following a consultation meeting held in September 2005 by HEFCE, the Arts and Humanities Research Council and the Economics and Social Science Research Council, bids were invited for collaborative centres in the identified strategic and vulnerable language areas. For the East Asian area, bids were solicited specifically for Chinese or Japanese, with a single winning bid signalled the preferred outcome, although in the case of Chinese the possibility was held out of two centres being supported. In the event, when the successful bids were announced in May 2006, there was one joint centre involving both Chinese and Japanese, based on Sheffield and Leeds universities and due to receive £4 million over five years, and a centre for Chinese only based on Oxford, Manchester and Bristol universities and due to receive £5 million over the same period. Korean studies did not feature at all in this process.[23] Given that Britain has considerable interests in Korea, both strategic and economic, this omission seems surprising and regrettable, but fits in with HEFCE's broad-brush approach of concentrating on what it sees as the main languages (Russian, Arabic, Chinese and Japanese) and letting the 'minor' languages (Korean, Persian, Turkish, etc.) fall to the individual institutions for support.[24]

Implications for the teaching of Korean in the UK

In the UK context it is very difficult to see Korean courses being viable outside an East Asian studies framework, except conceivably in specialist areas such as postgraduate-level translation. Even the two institutions offering undergraduate degrees in Korean, SOAS and Sheffield University, rely to a considerable extent on recruiting additional students to take Korean as a subsidiary or minor subject, and offering courses relating to Japan or China to their students majoring in Korean as options in order to provide choice and reduce the teaching burden on Korean studies staff.[25] It is noticeable that, primarily as a result of pressure on staff resources, courses in Korean tend to be less intensive than those in Japanese or Chinese and the final standard achieved in the language is lower. Bench-marking will make this discrepancy more visible, and may bring problems for Korean studies units involved in language teaching. Departments of East Asian studies struggle to achieve simultaneous viability in all three areas (teaching, research and finance) and with universities constantly raising the bar (demanding higher minimum enrolment figures for modules, higher research scores and higher contribution rates [i.e. profits]), it is difficult to envisage a more generous funding environment for Korean studies unless this comes from Korean sources.[26] In the longer term, the number of students applying for East Asian studies courses is growing[27] and to the extent that these departments are held back by low student numbers, these increases will help Korean studies too.

Although Chinese is now becoming more prominent as a result of economic and political factors, it is notable that in recent years Japanese studies have been more successful in recruiting students at both secondary school and university level. There are lessons in this for Korean studies. One is certainly the importance of marketing. Subjects do rise and fall according to fashion and image. We should not imagine that subjects are circumscribed by a natural level of interest determined by external or objective factors. Japanese organisations have been very successful in projecting a positive image of Japan, particularly among young people. For example, British schools have diversity requirements that often find expression in the project system. In these there is considerable discretion on the part of the teacher over the choice of topic. The Japan Foundation and the cultural section of the Japanese Embassy have been very active in providing project material boxes to schools on a loan basis, ensuring that many schools, both primary and secondary, carry out projects on Japan. Japanese has also had a particular appeal to young people, especially young males, interested in martial arts and animé or manga.[28] Korean popular culture has spread throughout East Asia in the form of the Hallyu 'Korean Wave', indicating at least a potential for export further afield.

Views from the World Koreanists Forum 2005

The papers were arranged by region and in the event the issues themselves tended to have a regional dimension. Problems of funding were a leitmotif running through the presentations of almost all the participants, though there were differences of emphasis here between those largely reliant on Korean funds and those in the market economy system dependent on attracting students for their income. The former group especially complained of the difficulty of making long-term plans based on short-term funding. This had been exacerbated by the 1997–9 financial crisis that brought home to universities just how fragile some of the funding was, particularly for Asian universities heavily dependent on private funding from Korean companies operating in their midst.

United States

Disregarding earlier Japanese or Chinese study of Korea, the United States has one of the longest-established and most extensive programmes of Korean studies outside the Korean peninsula. The earliest programme is said to have been at Columbia University, dating from 1932.[29] A paper by Edward Schultz of Hawai'i outlined developments at Hawai'i, whose Center for Korean Studies has "by far the greatest number of scholars of any department in the United States",[30] with 32 scholars listed. Formal language instruction programmes in Korean began in 1954 after the end of the Korean War and by 1968 were at a take-off point.[31] It was one of five universities designated as special centres for Korean studies (others were Columbia, Harvard, University of California Berkeley and the University of Washington). Ed Schultz indicated three basic requirements for a successful strategy: student demand, strong but consistent community support, and external support from Korea. His comment that "[s]tudent demand is at the base of any Korean studies program"[32] is a truism that was illustrated time and again by different speakers, especially from Western 'market-economy' universities. Hawai'i is of course fortunate in having a large ethnic Korean community to provide the first two of these requirements. As he says: "Korean studies has never had to justify its existence in Hawai'i."[33] One of the features of Korean studies in the US is its popularity with 'heritage' students from an ethnic Korean background, who form a high proportion of the enrolment on many campuses. Schultz illustrates his other requirements with the construction of the physical centre, a traditional building modelled on features of the Sudŏksa temple and the Kyŏngbok palace. This centre building was completed in 1980 with funds provided by the Republic of Korea, the State of Hawai'i and donations from the local community in roughly equal proportions.

A very different US perspective was offered in a paper entitled 'Controlling interests in Korean studies' by Denis Hart of Kent State University and Young Rae Oum.[34] This is part analysis, part exposé of the Korean studies scene in the US from the perspective of a non-Ivy League university. The authors consider the various interests: the Korean government, the US government, host universities, overseas Koreanists, and students in the field. The motivation of the South Korean government is clear: a "wish to use Korean studies to improve the images [sic] and political leverage of the Korean state in part by generating more knowledge, understanding and appreciation of Korea by non-Koreans."[35] The US government's interests are said to be even clearer: "to serve American interests as a hegemon first"[36] with the interests of the Korean people subordinated to this. For US host university administrators, education is increasingly "a commodity as opposed to a social or public service", hence their interests focus on "enrollment, endowments, corporate investments, and the 'bottom line'".[37]

Finally they identify a disparate group of individuals participating in the subject, who can be subdivided into the following. Firstly, a "Korean studies mafia" that controls access to the subject and its resources. These are "first generation 'white fathers' who recruit, mentor and anoint a selected few younger scholars, while promoting particular avenues of research, publications, dissertations and jobs within the field."[38] These are accused of first-world-centrism and using the considerable resources they control to advance personal agendas. The second group, Korean Americans, often act as native informants and in their writings pander to the prejudices of their white audience by presenting Korea in orientalist 'Other' terms in order to secure their positions. "They could be seen as the spear bearers of orientalism."[39] Native Korean scholars in the US are presented as marginalised and ignored by the preceding two groups, partly as a result of language and partly through their powerlessness. Within this group is a set compared to the 'organic intellectuals' of Gramsci, which is truly radical and iconoclastic in its willingness to reinterpret key themes in Korean history, such as the civil war and relations with the US. This paper also notes the importance of enrolments and the key role of 'heritage' students.

The effect of this situation has been to skew Korean government support towards Ivy League institutions as the best avenues to influence US opinion formers, but these institutions are precisely those that support conservative policies based on perceived US self-interest. The paper suggests that some such élite schools were strong supporters of cold war policies that have helped damage and divide Korea. The paper also takes issue with the Korean government and the Korea Foundation for showing "a clear preference for white scholars"[40] and bias against ethnic Koreans, especially females, in their grant-funding policies. In order to resolve all the above problems, Hart and Young suggest the development of E-plaza as a cyber-space open forum for interaction between Americans and Koreans on the basis of equality, not an orientalist unequal relationship

East Asia[41]

Korea and China have traditionally enjoyed a much closer relationship with each other than with any other state, characterised by Korea's use of the term *sadae*.[42] Japan's colonisation of Korea and the presence of a large number of Japanese of Korean origin has changed this situation, but relations between both Koreas and China are marked by a level of mutual respect and cordiality that arguably transcends Korea's other relationships. The area of China bordering Russia and North Korea has an Autonomous Korean prefecture with a Korean ('China's Korean nationality') population of 40 per cent. This is the location of a private Korean (joint-venture) university, Yanbian University of Science and Technology, established in 1989 (Yanbian University is a national university founded in 1949). The re-establishment of diplomatic relations between the People's Republic of China and the Republic of Korea in 1992 has transformed Korean studies in China. There are eight research and teaching institutes for Korean studies, mostly founded around 1992–3 (within Northeast Normal University, 1992; in the Chinese Academy of Social Sciences, 1993; at Shandong University, 1993; in Fudan University Shanghai, 1992; at Zhejiang University, 1993; in Beijing University, date unknown; and at Renmin University, 1996). An exception to this is, unsurprisingly, Yanbian University's Research Centre of North and South Korean Studies, founded in 1989. Most universities focus on contemporary social science subjects—politics, economics, law and international relations—but Yanbian is again, unsurprisingly, more orientated towards culture and history, as are Shandong, Zhejiang and, to some extent, Beijing. These universities and institutions are either in areas with traditional strong links to Korea and lie in northeast or eastern China, or are leading national institutions which aim to be comprehensive in their coverage. Key topics for research are the democratisation of Korea in the 1980s, economic development, China-Korea relations and Korean peninsula problems. The centres are largely dependent on Korean sources, much of which is private Korean financial group funding and other short-term funds that could leave them very exposed.

The paper on Japan indicates that in 2002, Korean language courses were taught in just under half of all Japanese four-year universities. For comparison, almost all universities offer English and around 80 per cent offer French, Chinese and German, but only 35 per cent Spanish and 28 per cent Russian. However, only 15 or so Japanese universities have specialist units teaching Korean studies. While other languages were static or falling, the trend for Korean was upwards, with student numbers at the respondent's university (Osaka University of Economics and Law) rising rapidly between 2003 and 2005 to eclipse French and German, putting Korean third behind English and Chinese.[43]

Southeast Asia

There were programmes represented from Thailand, Vietnam, Indonesia and Malaysia. Thailand has the most extensive programmes: these date from 1986 and currently involve 17 institutions offering some level of Korean studies, including four universities offering Korean language at elective, minor and major level. The 17 have a total of 46 members of staff, 27 of them Koreans, almost all supported by Korean sources, principally the Korea International Cooperation Agency (which had 19 volunteers teaching in Thailand). One university, Burapha, is receiving support from 14 Korean agencies.

Vietnam established diplomatic relations in 2002 and has eight universities with Korean studies departments but only one, Vietnam National University: University of

Social Sciences and Humanities, with two branches in Hanoi and Ho Chi Minh City, teaches an actual programme. It is short of everything.

In Malaysia, just one university, the University of Malaya, has a Korean programme offering a BA degree majoring in Korean, located at its Department of East Asian Studies. It is sponsored by the Korea Foundation, Korea Research Foundation and five Korean companies. It is short of staff, has difficulty recruiting qualified staff, and needs more funds to develop all areas: teaching, research, library, textbooks, staff and student exchanges.

The University of Indonesia offers Korean as a minor subject, and was due to start a Korean studies programme in 2006–07, but as of autumn 2005 had no full-time teaching staff and needed funding for everything.

Oceania[44]

Although the Hallyu 'Korean Wave', which has seen Korean popular culture spread throughout East Asia, has not influenced Australia and New Zealand to the same extent, there has been increasing interest in Korea, but with economic and security issues behind this rather than cultural ones. The Australian government's decision in 1994 to include Korean among four Asian languages to be taught in high schools gave the subject a considerable boost. Korean studies, which date back to the 1980s, went through a lean period from the mid-1980s to the mid-1990s, but in Australia there are now at least four universities offering three- or four-year undergraduate degree courses in Korean, and one in New Zealand, at Auckland. The biggest centre is at Australian National University (ANU), where the Korean Studies Centre was set up 1994. It is supported by the Korea Foundation but no other external sources and has a professor, three lecturers and a number of language instructors. Resources are excellent, with a Korean collection in the National Library of 45,000 monographs and 1,500 serials on hand and a specialist collection in the Menzies Library at ANU. There have been relatively few 'heritage' students in the past, but several universities are introducing courses for students from Korean-speaking backgrounds.

The general pattern for honours courses in Korean is that students take a single Korean-language course in each of nine semesters over three years, with five hours a week of instruction, plus a specified number of background courses on Korea or East Asia. Courses allow for a year to be spent in Korea, typically in year three. For example, the ANU course of Bachelor of Asian Studies (Korean) is the specialist Korean course with a required year in Korea, a total of eight language courses over the three years at ANU plus background courses. A trend noted is the diminishing teaching hours which have accompanied the greater emphasis on research, with universities now tending to reduce teaching loads from five to four per week for language courses to meet the demands of the Performance-based Research Funding

System. A common complaint is the lack of appropriate language teaching textbooks, which are felt to be culture- and system-specific to an extent that makes materials from other regions unsuitable for use in Australia and New Zealand.

Europe and the Middle East

This section included papers from Kazakhstan,[45] Egypt,[46] Russia[47] and seven western European institutions. Reports from these countries touched upon almost all the opportunities and problems and all the economic, political and social issues facing Korean studies. There are half a million ethnic Koreans living in the Commonwealth of Independent States, with 400,000 of these in Central Asia, and thriving trade with Korea brings good employment opportunities for graduates in Korean. Hence the Kazakh State University of International Relations and World Languages has 150 students of Korean, and in Far Eastern Russia there are around 100 students each in Khabarovsk, Ussuriysk, Vladivostok and Sakhalin. These latter have very intensive five-year teaching programmes including high-level language work and extensive background study.

In many ways Egypt occupies a polar opposite situation with few Koreans, no university language courses and limited contact. Interest was stimulated in the 1990s by Korea's economic miracle and democratisation. How had a country which 25 years before had lagged behind Egypt by almost every measure suddenly leapt massively ahead? With minor exceptions (the first being a report by Boutros Ghali on Korea and the UN dating from 1951), Korean studies dated from the establishment of the Center for Asian Studies at Cairo University in 1994. Study of Korea focuses on social science issues, is highly dependent on Korean funding, and so far efforts to develop Korean language courses have not been successful.

In Western Europe two trends inimical to traditional Korean studies have been prominent. The first is a shift from an arts and humanities focus, involving the study of traditional Korea, culture and classical language, to a social sciences focus on modern language, politics, economics and business. The second is a demand-led consumerist approach to courses, which makes it very hard for smaller, higher-cost subjects to survive. Governments are trying to increase participation in higher education without increasing overall budgets, forcing unit costs down and obliging universities to look for economies of scale. Increased measurement of research outputs with financial rewards for successful researchers is also having an impact on teaching-intensive subjects. Added to this, in much of Europe the Bologna Process[48] is leading to wholesale changes in university structures, adding a further destabilising factor. It is countries where the market-led approach has gone furthest, such as the UK and Germany, where Korean studies has suffered the greatest cutbacks, while in neighbouring countries with a more centralist approach, such as France and Austria, the subject is thriving. All of these changes are tending to have a negative effect on the student's proficiency in Korean by the end of the course. Sergey Kurbanov's description of teaching at St Petersburg State University met with incredulity. Had he been misunderstood? Was he really claiming that second-year students were expected to write original research papers based on Korean-language sources? Yes, he was. And what happened to those who failed? They are thrown out. Can you really afford to throw out students? A shrug. "Why not?" A different world. Students in the shortened post-Bologna courses of western Russia have 476 hours of Korean language tuition in the first year, out of a total of 619 contact hours. This compares with, for example, 104 hours of Korean-language instruction per year on Korean courses at Western market-oriented, portion-control-conscious universities. A further aspect of Russian idiosyncrasy is a determination to continue to teach translation, because this is a skill graduates need, rather than adopting the communicative-functional spoken language approach used elsewhere, including Korea. A result of this is that the Russians have to produce their own teaching materials.

Afterword

Although the Tokto/Takeshima argument for an increase in Korean government spending on promoting Korean studies overseas may seem over-simplistic, it is not without merit. Korea's profile in many countries of the world is very low, especially in comparison with its neighbours China and Japan. Japan has been very successful in generating interest by targeting foreign schools with information and materials. Japanese popular culture has certain features that are very attractive to some young people, but Korea too has been successful in exporting aspects of its popular culture, at least to neighbouring countries. Furthermore, Korea's spending on promoting Korean culture abroad appears low compared to other countries, not just Japan.[49]

Only in particularly favourable circumstances, for example a plentiful supply of 'heritage' students (as in Hawai'i) or good employment opportunities (Thailand, Far Eastern Russia), does Korean attract large numbers of students. Alternative survival strategies (cutting back on teaching hours, linking Korean language study to more vocationally relevant social science courses, fitting Korean studies into an East Asian studies framework for more economical, bigger-group teaching) may help but with the pressures on universities to cut costs, the role of Korean financial support is likely to continue to be crucial for the development and survival of Korean studies in many countries. Given the relatively small sums involved, it seems like good value for Korea.

Notes

1. Held 17–19 October 2005 at the Academy for Korean Studies (AKS), Seoul, jointly organised by the AKS and the Korea Foundation, and sponsored by the Ministry of Education and Human Resources Development, the Korea Research Foundation and Samsung Electronics.
2. Posted on 19 April 2005 on "Koreanstudies-bounces@koreaweb.ws on behalf of Don Starr".
3. This was published in the *World Koreanists Forum 2005: Proceedings*. Seoul: Association for Korean Studies, 2005: 201–12. I should like to thank Professor James Grayson and Dr Judith Cherry from Sheffield, Dr Jay Lewis from Oxford, Dr Jaehoon Yeon from SOAS and Professor Keith Pratt from Durham for their invaluable guidance and assistance.
4. Appeared in *Digital Chosun Ilbo* (English Edition), 29 March 2005. See: http://english.chosun.com/w21data/html/news/200503/200503290024.html, accessed on 18 April 2005.
5. We were told at several points in the forum that the AKS was to be heir to the Korea Research Foundation's annual governmental subvention of 1.5 million. This caused a certain amount of puzzlement (in wŏn it was the equivalent of a good meal for a couple of merchant bankers) until someone questioned the figure and it was explained that this was in US dollars.
6. http://english.chosun.com/w21data/html/news/200503/200503300024.html, accessed on 18 April 2005.
7. KOICA's mission is providing aid for developing countries.
8. In the decade from 1989 to 1998, public funding per student fell from a starting index of 100 to 63. (Data taken from 'A tale of two countries: higher education "incorporation" in the UK and Japan', a Daiwa Anglo-Japanese Foundation Lecture delivered on 1 February 2005 by Professor Sir David Watson and Professor Fujio Ohmori.) This drop followed the Conservative government's decision to abolish the binary divide between universities and polytechnics in the UK higher education system, and to allow polytechnics to convert themselves into universities, doubling the number of universities. The traditional universities, much better funded than the polytechnics, were forced to 'level-down'.
9. A special HEFCE minority-subject funding system applied from 1991 to 2005, with earmarked funds available for a group of subjects recruiting broadly fewer than 100 students nationally.
10. 'Evaluation of HEFCE funding for minority subjects: A report to HEFCE by Universitas'. HEFCE 2005/02, at http://www.hefce.ac.uk/pubs/rdreports/2005/rd03_05/rd03_05b.doc
11. RAEs, formerly termed research selectivity exercises, were conducted in 1986, 1989, 1992, 1996 and 2001, with the next due in 2008.
12. For staff in post on the qualifying date the university receives funding according to the RAE grade for the rest of that RAE period, i.e. for six years in the case of the 2001 RAE, whether or not the staff are still employed there. The 2001 RAE graded research as 1, 2, 3a, 3b, 4, 5 or 5*; in 2001 only 4, 5 or 5* attracted additional funding, roughly at the rate of £7000 per annum for a 4, rising to £30,000 per annum for a 5*. A member of staff working in a 5* department on the qualifying date in 2001 will bring in a total of over £180,000 to that department over the 2002–08 period.

13. In the 2001 RAE, none of the leading East Asian studies departments managed a volume measure of A (i.e. almost all research-active staff entered for the assessment), with most on B or C; for history at those same universities, half were A and the rest all B.
14. See www.dfes.gov.uk/languagesstrategy for the UK official National Languages Strategy. The UK government also supports CILT, the Centre for Information on Language Teaching and Research, which in 2003 merged with the Languages National Training Organisation to form the National Centre for Languages.
15. Private comment to the writer by a HEFCE executive.
16. By contrast, in nursing no university achieved the highest grade and over 75 per cent fell below a grade 4. As a result HEFCE introduced a special system of funding nursing, and a few other chronic low-scoring subjects, for 3a and 3b levels of research.
17. This does not apply to departments of classics, which have successfully promoted an image of embodying the UK's cultural roots, and hence having higher value than 'foreign' modern languages; there is also the Oxbridge culture of regarding classics as a rigorous academic discipline, reflected in the epithet 'Greats'. At the time that Durham University decided to close down East Asian studies, part of the savings were 'invested' in classics, a subject perceived by senior management as having better future prospects.
18. In the case of classics, only three units out of the 26 assessed fell below a grade 4, and six achieved 5*.
19. http://www.hefce.ac.uk/pubs/hefce/2005/05_24/ p.6.
20. The Common European Framework of Reference for Languages (CEF) was established by the Council of Europe to provide a common standard for defining linguistic proficiency in foreign languages; it has six grades, A1 to C2. The UK Language Ladder is a 14-grade system referenced against the CEF. See: http://www.cilt.org.uk/qualifications/cef.htm
21. In the case of East Asia, the British Association for Korean Studies, British Association for Chinese Studies and British Association for Japanese Studies.
22. HEFCE is not willing to recognise that its undergraduate funding model, which pays universities the same amount for teaching all languages regardless of whether it is *ab initio* Chinese or post-A level French, is flawed.
23. Unlike Chinese and Japanese, Korean studies has been eligible for strategic and vulnerable subject undergraduate funding, but this is only shown as being provided to Sheffield in 1991 and 1995, not in the 2000 bidding round. See: 'Evaluation of HEFCE funding for minority subjects: A report to HEFCE by Universitas', p.32 at http://www.hefce.ac.uk/pubs/rdreports/2005/rd03_05/. SOAS is subject to a separate funding system which recognises its strategic and vulnerable subject role.
24. The five centres receiving HEFCE funding for five years as announced in May 2006 are: 1. The Centre for East European Language Based Area Studies (University College London with the Universities of Oxford and Birmingham), 2. The British Interuniversity China Centre (Universities of Oxford, Bristol and Manchester), 3. The White Rose East Asia Centre (Japan and China; the Universities of Leeds and Sheffield), 4. Eastern Europe and Russia Research Centre (University of Glasgow in collaboration with the Universities of St Andrews, Aberdeen, Edinburgh, Paisley, Strathclyde, Newcastle and Nottingham. 5. A centre studying

the Arabic-speaking world (University of Edinburgh in partnership with the Universities of Durham and Manchester). See: http://www.hefce.ac.uk/news/hefce/2006/esrc.htm

25. As of October 2006, the full-time staff numbers in Korean language and culture teaching units are: three at SOAS, four at Sheffield and two at Oxford. These figures do not include a number of specialists in other departments. For example, SOAS also has a Senior Lecturer in the Department of Art and Archaeology specialising in Korean, a Reader in Korean Studies and Music in the Department of Music, and a Lecturer in Politics specialising in Korea in the Department of Politics and International Studies. The SOAS Centre of Korean Studies lists nine members of staff.

26. Dr Lewis's post in Oxford was secured through the agreement of colleagues in Japanese studies to sacrifice a Japanese post in order to support Korean, but such generosity is exceptional.

27. *The Guardian* reported in early 2006 a 66 per cent increase in applicants for Chinese courses compared to the previous year. A year-end figure provided by the British Embassy in Beijing in personal correspondence on 29 September 2006 was that the latest UCAS figures for 2006/07 applications had "increased by nearly 60% to 788". Details for earlier years are given on the UCAS website, e.g. for 2005 see: http://www.ucas.com/figures/archive/applications/2005

28. This has in some cases helped turn round the student gender balance of departments of East Asian studies from being predominantly female to attracting equal numbers of males and females, something that is attractive to all students. There was a 2:1 preponderance of female students studying Chinese in Durham in the 1970s and 1980s; in recent years for Chinese and Japanese it has been more balanced, though currently it is reversed with more male students.

29. Michale Namkil Kim, 'The trend in the development of Korean textbooks in North America', *The World Koreanists Forum 2005: Proceedings*. Seoul: Association for Korean Studies, 2005:117

30. See: http://www.hawaii.edu/korea/pages/faculty/index.htm, accessed 16 August 2006.

31. Edward J. Schultz, 'Recent trends in Korean studies in North America: Korean studies in Hawai'i as a model', *World Koreanists Forum 2005: Proceedings*. Seoul: Association for Korean Studies, 2005:105–14.

32. ibid.:112.

33. ibid.:107.

34. Denis Hart and Young Rae Oum, 'Controlling interests in Korean studies', *World Koreanists Forum 2005:Proceedings*. Seoul: Association for Korean Studies, 2005:91–104.

35. ibid.:93.

36. ibid.:94.

37. ibid.:94.

38. ibid.:95.

39. ibid.:95.

40. ibid.:98.

41. The following is taken from Yue Chen's 'Korean studies in Chinese universities', *World Koreanists Forum 2005: Proceedings*. Seoul: Association for Korean Studies, 2005:11–16, and Song Jae-mog's 'Recent trend of Korean studies in Japanese universities and development strategy of Overseas Korean Studies Association', *Proceedings*:1–9.

42. Meaning 'serving the great' and used by Chosŏn-dynasty Korea to describe relations with Ming-dynasty China.

43. Song Jae-mog, 'Recent trend of Korean studies in Japanese universities and development strategy of Overseas Korean Studies Association', *World Koreanists Forum 2005: Proceedings*. Seoul: Association for Korean Studies, 2005:1–9.

44. Based on Tatiana Gabroussenko, 'Evaluation and feedback on international support programs of related Korean institutions', *World Koreanists Forum 2005: Proceedings*. Seoul: Association for Korean Studies, 2005:59–69; Changzoo Song, 'Korean studies curriculum and development of textbook in Oceania: current status and some suggestions', *Proceedings*:71–80; Pankaj Mohan, 'Korean studies at the University of Sydney', *Proceedings*:81–89.

45. Nelly Pak, 'Trends of Korean studies in Central Asia and Russia and development strategy', *World Koreanists Forum 2005: Proceedings*. Seoul: Association for Korean Studies, 2005:173–80.

46. Mohammed El-Sayed Selim, 'The status of Korean studies in Egypt', *World Koreanists Forum 2005: Proceedings*. Seoul: Association for Korean Studies, 2005:181–99.

47. S. O. Kurbanov, 'Trend of Korean studies curriculum in Russian universities: development of Korean studies textbooks in Russia', *World Koreanists Forum 2005: Proceedings*. Seoul: Association for Korean Studies, 2005:235–44.

48. See: http://www.coe.int/T/DG4/HigherEducation/EHEA2010/BolognaPedestrians_en.asp

49. For example, in the 2005/06 fiscal year, the British Council received a grant from the British government of £186 million, or around US$335 million, compared to the *Chosun Ilbo* figure of US$5.4 million cited above (p.23) for Korean government expenditure. See: http://www.britishcouncil.org/home-about-us-governance-funding.htm.

HWANG BYUNGKI AND NORTH-SOUTH MUSICAL EXCHANGE

Andrew P. Killick

In October and December 1990, North and South Korea sent parties of musicians to each other in an exchange of musical performances intended to express the will for unification. On other occasions, one side has sent a musical delegation to the other, but this is the only time to date there has been a reciprocal exchange of such visits in close succession. This pair of events has been described by Han Myŏnghŭi, Song Hyejin and Yun Chunggang in their book *Uri kugak 100 nyŏn* (100 years of Korean traditional music) as "the most noteworthy cultural exchange between North and South since partition" (Han Myŏnghŭi *et al.*, 2001:352).

In reviewing the 1990 North-South musical exchange, I will concentrate on the role of composer and *kayagŭm* player Hwang Byungki (Hwang Pyŏnggi; b. 1936), arguably the most prominent figure in the exchange as a whole, since he led the South Korean delegation to P'yŏngyang and organised the Seoul concerts, performed his own works in both events, and composed two new pieces for the occasion. My information comes mainly from interviews with Hwang Byungki in 2005, from his own published writings on the subject (Hwang Byungki, 1994a, 1994b), from copies of his musical manuscripts, and from a North Korean commemorative volume which he kindly gave me (produced by P'yŏngyang Tŭngdaesa, 1990).

The two pieces Hwang wrote for P'yŏngyang are not often heard outside Korea, but they shed an interesting light both on Hwang Byungki as a composer and on the possibilities and challenges for North-South musical dialogue. Although this paper is not intended for a specialist music audience, I would like to be specific about the musical features of these pieces, in the hope that a musicologist's perspective can contribute something new to the discussion of informal diplomacy on the Korean peninsula.

The first event was the *Pŏmminjok t'ongil ŭmakhoe* (Pan-Korean unification concerts) held in P'yŏngyang from 18 to 23 October 1990. In this lavish music festival, no fewer that eighteen groups took part, representing not only the two Koreas but Korean diaspora communities in places as far flung as North America,

Germany, China, Japan, and various republics of the former Soviet Union. Most of these groups performed Western-style music, as we might guess from the festival's logo, which showed a map of the Korean peninsula encircled by a treble clef with staff lines passing through it (fig. 1). We might also be tempted to link the emphasis on Western-style music with the chair of the organising committee, Yun Isang (1917–95), a composer who wrote mainly for Western classical instruments, although he strove to evoke elements of traditional Korean music. But it was Yun who invited Hwang Byungki to lead the South Korean contingent, specifically requesting that the group perform traditional Korean music from the time before partition because this music had not been maintained in the North.

Hwang assembled a party of fourteen musicians whom he considered the best in their field, including three designated holders of Important Intangible Cultural Properties (*chungyo muhyŏng munhwajae*) and the entire Kim Duk Soo SamulNori percussion quartet. He planned a concert programme for the group that included a number of pieces evoking the theme of reunification: for instance, the *p'ansori* excerpt performed by O Chŏngsuk described the reunion of the heroine and her father at the end of the *Song of Sim Ch'ŏng*. Of Hwang's own compositions, he chose the kayagŭm solo *Pidan'gil* (The Silk Road) for its theme of exchange between two civilisations, and the song *Kohyang-ŭi tal* (Moon of my hometown) for its theme of longing for home. He also composed a new song which was given its première

Fig.1. Logo for *Pŏmminjok t'ongil ŭmakhoe* (Pan-Korean unification concerts), P'yŏngyang, 18–23 October 1990 (P'yŏngyangTŭngdaesa,1990:1)

in P'yŏngyang by the only performer of Western music in the South Korean party, soprano Yun Insuk. This was *Uri-nŭn hana* (We are one), and it reveals much about Hwang's approach to the musical exchange with North Korea in the way it departs from his usual compositional style.

Uri-nŭn hana can be heard in Yun Insuk's performance on the compact disc of the same title (Yun Insuk, 2000; see Discography). The song has no text other than the words *Uri-nŭn hana*, which are repeated many times, alternating with short passages of wordless singing. Given that *uri* so often means Koreans as a nation, it would be easy to interpret this text as a mantra affirming that North and South Korea are one. Hwang told me that he intended the song to include this meaning, but that he also meant *uri* in a broader sense, embracing the whole human race. He had long believed that man's inhumanity to man was caused by failing to see the human race as one, and he had harboured the idea of writing a piece on this theme for many years. But the form in which the piece eventually emerged was very much moulded by the context in which it was to be given its first performance. We can see this not only in the choice of text but in the musical style as well.

This becomes clear when we compare *Uri-nŭn hana* with the music Hwang had been composing shortly before he was invited to P'yŏngyang. After some avant-garde ventures in the 1970s such as *Migung* (The labyrinth, 1975; recorded on the Hwang Byungki CD, 1993a) and *Jasi* (Night watch, 1978; to be recorded on Hwang's next CD), Hwang's compositions became more consistently focused on traditional Korean musical resources. This tendency perhaps reached its peak in 1987 with *Namdo hwansanggok* (Southern fantasy) for kayagŭm zither and *changgo* hourglass drum (recorded on the Hwang Byungki CD, 1993b), which is rather close in style to the traditional genre kayagŭm *sanjo*, a type of extended instrumental solo with drum accompaniment. *Namdo hwansanggok* is characteristic of Hwang Byungki's music in a number of ways: it is written for a small number of traditional Korean instruments; it is inspired by a traditional Korean genre; it is thin in texture with only sparing use of harmony; its rhythms are subtle and irregular, and its overall mood contemplative. Some of these characteristics also appear in *Uri-nŭn hana*, but not in such obvious ways.

Hwang was aware that, while traditional music in South Korea had been both preserved and developed, in the North there was little concern with preservation, and traditional genres had been either developed to suit the needs of a modern socialist state or abandoned altogether. North Korean development of traditional music in many respects emulated Western classical music: for instance, in extending the pitch range and technical capabilities of instruments; in aiming for a pure, clear tone in contrast to the rough-edged timbres of much traditional Korean music; and in making free use of functional harmony (Howard, 2002: 960–63). Hwang designed *Uri-nŭn hana* to speak to audiences accustomed to this acculturated North Korean music. Although he used the traditional changgo drum (played with the bare hands rather than using a stick on one or both heads as in traditional music) and provided a short introduction on the Korean clay ocarina *hun*, he wrote the song for a Western-style soprano with a thick chordal accompaniment on the organ that was very uncharacteristic of his previous compositional style.

On closer examination, however, the Western sound of *Uri-nŭn hana* turns out to be largely a matter of instrumentation (the Western-style voice and the organ, which Hwang says provides just "atmosphere"), and in its musical construction the piece is markedly Korean. Its overall structure does not follow the 'recursive' principle so common in Western music, whereby earlier material returns in later sections. Instead, it moves on from one idea to another with several increases in tempo and a concluding slow passage, much like traditional sanjo. The introduction on the *hun* is not thematically connected to the rest of the piece, but serves mainly to invoke the associations of this instrument with the earth or land (since it is made of clay) and with the land of Korea in particular (since it sounds markedly different from Chinese and other ocarinas). Although notated in the key of F minor, the piece does not use the 'leading note' (E-natural) that would be essential to that tonality in Western music, but is in fact written in a melodic mode resembling the *kyemyŏnjo* of Korean folk music. Its rhythmic structure in 6/4 time derives from the twelve beats of *chungmori*, one of the *changdan* or 'rhythmic cycles' of traditional Korean music, and its use of the changgo for rhythmic accompaniment is shared with most traditional genres. Its vocal writing evokes traditional song styles such as *sijo* and p'ansori by using vibrato only on certain notes, and sometimes on less than the full length of a note.

If these Korean musical elements might be taken to encourage a narrowly national reading of *Uri-nŭn hana*, the Western elements might suggest Hwang's broader meaning of the whole human race being one. The combination of Korean musical elements and an international musical language might also stand as an emblem for the coming together of ethnic Koreans from around the world in the P'yŏngyang Pan-Korean unification concerts. At any rate, Hwang told me that the piece was particularly well received by the North Korean press, although they perhaps predictably interpreted its message as referring specifically to the unity of the Korean people.

Another song that Hwang composed for P'yŏngyang was *T'ongil-ŭi kil* (The road of unification), written in collaboration with North Korean composer Sŏng Tongch'un, although the two composers did not actually meet until the song was finished. The creative process began when Hwang was sent a number of North Korean poems, from which he was asked to choose one for setting to music. He chose Ri Sŏngch'ŏl's poem *T'ongil-ŭi kil* because it seemed relatively apolitical, urging all Koreans to pool their strength and walk hand in hand towards unification, without indicating the specific form that a unified Korea would take:

*Uri kyŏrye taedaero ogo kadŏn kil
san-i nop'a ogaji mot hanunga?
Ne-ga ogo nae-ga kal t'ongil-ŭi kil-ŭn
uri sŏro son chapko yŏro nagaja.*

On the road by which our people used to come and go,
is the hill too high to cross?
Hand in hand, let's go forth and open
a road of unification for you to come and for me to go.

Hwang composed a first draft of the melody and sent it to Sŏng Tongch'un for revision. While he no longer remembers the details of the changes that Sŏng made, his recollection is that they were fairly slight, and that they tended to make the song more "popular" (*taejungjŏk*) in style, whereas his original version had been too "high-brow" (here Hwang used the English word) for its intended purpose. He readily accepted most of Sŏng's changes, but they had difficulty in reaching agreement over the setting of the title phrase *t'ongil-ŭi kil*. They discussed the problem over the phone and settled on a compromise, and when they eventually met, the two composers signed the score. During the festivities in P'yŏngyang, they sang the song as a duet before getting the whole company to sing it together.

Like *Uri-nŭn hana*, *T'ongil-ŭi kil* is strikingly different in style from most of Hwang's music. In contrast to his usual rhythmic subtlety, it has the four-square structure of a simple hymn, with four lines each four bars long and nearly identical to each other in rhythm. It has much internal repetition, with a melodic form of AABB' (where B and B' have the same beginning but different endings). Although it has no written-out accompaniment, it is clearly conceived with harmony in mind, and in P'yŏngyang a harmonic accompaniment was improvised on the accordion, very skillfully according to Hwang. Yet also like *Uri-nŭn hana*, it evokes traditional Korean music in its use of a six-beat metre (multiples of three beats being highly characteristic of Korean music) and a melodic mode that resembles a Western minor key but lacks the raised leading note. Because of these features, Hwang feels that the melody sounds very traditional although it can easily be learnt and sung by those unaccustomed to traditional Korean singing—which includes most of those present at the P'yŏngyang festival and most ethnic Koreans worldwide.

On his return from P'yŏngyang, Hwang set about organising a return visit by musicians from North Korea (though not from the various diaspora communities that had been represented in P'yŏngyang). This became the *Songnyŏn t'ongil chŏnt'ong ŭmakhoe* (Year-end traditional music concerts for unification), a series of concerts held in Seoul in December 1990, in which musicians from the two Koreas performed on the same stage. Hwang wrote about both the P'yŏngyang and Seoul concerts in two magazine articles that were later reprinted in his 1994 book *Kip'ŭn pam, kŭ kayagŭm sori* (The sound of the kayagŭm in the dead of night; Hwang Byungki, 1994a, 1994b). He noted that the North and South Korean participants appeared to approach the concerts with different expectations. The South Koreans tended to regard them as pure musical events, an opportunity to transcend the political conditions on the peninsula and share a common Korean identity on a cultural level. Thus, Han, Song and Yun in *Uri kugak 100 nyŏn* state that the exchange was judged to have "highlighted the national cultural homogeneity between North and South" (Han Myŏnghŭi *et al.*, 2001:353). But according to Hwang (1994a), opinions were divided as to whether the concerts showed that North and South Korea still shared a single musical tradition or whether, on the contrary, they showed that the tradition had taken such different paths in the two Koreas that it would be difficult to recover the original unity. Moreover, he suggests that even to ask this question shows a South Korean way of thinking that would not make sense to the participants from the North. To them, the musical exchange was essentially a political event, significant in exhibiting and promoting the will for unification regardless of the compatibility or even the quality of North and South Korean music. Thus, North Korean newspaper reports did not even mention whether the music was good or not, let alone whether North and South Korean musical forms were homogeneous or heterogeneous, but concentrated solely on the mood of longing for unification. Again, at the North Korean musicians' suggestion, the first Seoul concert ended with all the performers coming on stage together to sing An Byŏngwŏn's unification anthem, *Uri-ŭi sowŏn-ŭn t'ongil* (Our wish is for unification; recorded on the Yun Insuk CD, 2000). At the end of the song, the North Korean musicians shouted the slogan *choguk t'ongil* ('unify the homeland'). The next day, the South Korean performers, who wanted to keep the focus on music, insisted on changing the song to *Arirang*, and after a long argument the North Korean contingent gave in. Such incidents suggest that, despite the conciliatory gesture between North and South that the musical exchange implied, in some respects the two sides were at cross-purposes, and no very substantial outcome could be expected.

What in fact was the outcome? It would be difficult to argue, after this passage of time, that the 1990 musical exchange has brought the two Koreas any closer to unification. But within the realm of music, it appears to have had some effects. Hwang Byungki believes that in North Korea, it has led the authorities to attach more importance to traditional music, while in the South, it marked the beginning of an influx of North Korean elements into South Korean *ch'angjak kugak* (newly composed music for traditional instruments) and *kugak* fusion music. These elements include modified instruments with more than the traditional number of strings or, in the case of wind instruments, with metal keywork to make additional pitches available, as well as actual music by North Korean composers which can now be freely performed in the South. North Korean instruments and compositions often reach South Korea by way of the Yŏnbyŏn Korean Autonomous Region in China, where South Korean musicians travel to learn about North Korean music. Thus, each side has taken on something of the other's musical culture, and at least to that extent, the 1990 musical exchange has brought the two Koreas closer.

Han, Song and Yun predict that cultural and artistic exchanges will play an important role in future progress towards unification (Han Myŏnghŭi *et al.*, 2001:353). There may be some support for this view in the importance that both Koreas attached to the role of music. Hwang Byungki recalls that although the musical gathering in P'yŏngyang coincided with other unification-oriented events such as North-South football matches, summit meetings, and reunions of family members separated by the partition of Korea, it was the musical events that seemed to be in the brightest spotlight. On the South Korean side, it may be significant that a group of musicians were among the first private citizens to be allowed to visit North Korea since partition. At the very least, I suggest, the 1990 musical exchange shows that, if we are interested in informal diplomacy between North and South Korea, it is worth paying attention to music.

Editor's note: All translations from the Korean (titles, quotations, verse) are by the author. The only original English-language titles are those for Hwang Byungki's two albums, listed below.

References

Han Myŏnghŭi, with Song Hyejin and Yu Chunggang, 2001. *Uri kugak 100 nyŏn* [100 years of Korean traditional music]. Seoul: Hyŏnamsa

Howard, Keith, 2002. 'Contemporary genres', in Robert C. Provine, Yoshihiko Tokumaru and J. Lawrence Witzleben (eds), *Garland Encyclopedia of World Music*, vol. 7: *East Asia*. New York: Garland: 951–74

Hwang Byungki (Hwang Pyŏnggi), 1994a. '"*Ŭmakhoe*"-*e taehan nambuk-ŭi ijilsŏng*' [The heterogeneity of North and South with regard to concerts], in *Kip'ŭn pam, kŭ kayagŭm sori* [The sound of the *kayagŭm* in the dead of night]. Seoul: P'ulpit:144–48

——, 1994b. '*P'yŏngyang pŏmminjok t'ongil ŭmakhoe-ŭi twit iyagi*' [Afterword on the P'yŏngyang pan-Korean unification concerts], in *Kip'ŭn pam, kŭ kayagŭm sori* [The sound of the *kayagŭm* in the dead of night]. Seoul: P'ulpit:149–51

P'yŏngyang Tŭngdaesa, 1990. *Pŏmminjok t'ongil ŭmakhoe* [Pan-Korean unification music concerts]. P'yŏngyang: P'yŏngyang Tŭngdaesa

Discography

Hwang Byungki (Hwang Pyŏnggi), 1993a. *Hwang Pyŏnggi che-3 kayagŭm chakp'umjip* [Published English title: Kayagum Masterpieces Vol. 3 by Hwang Byung-Ki]. Compact disc. Seoul: Sung Eum (Sŏngŭm) DS0036

——, 1993b. *Hwang Pyŏnggi che-4 kayagŭm chakp'umjip* [Published English title: Kayagum Masterpieces Vol. 4 by Hwang Byung-Ki]. Compact disc. Seoul: Sung Eum (Sŏngŭm) DS0037

Yun Insuk, 2000. *Uri-nŭn hana: Yun Insuk minjok yŏmwŏn sŏngakkokchip* [We are one: Yun Insuk's collection of vocal pieces on the longing of the nation]. Compact disc. Seoul: Sinnara NSSRCD-024

THE KAESŎNG ARCHAEOLOGICAL PROJECT

DAVID LAKIN

Introduction

The author visited Kaesŏng as a representative of the Museum of London. His paper sketches out the proposals made at the time of his visit for an archaeological survey of Kaesŏng and its hinterland. In presenting his observations, he will repeat a couple of caveats: he is in no way a specialist in Korean archaeology; and the proposed archaeological project described here has yet to take place.

So how did the Museum of London become involved in an archaeological project in the Democratic People's Republic of Korea?

In the summer of 2002, Dr Tony Michell of Euro-Asian Business Consultancy came to the Museum of London Archaeology Service (MoLAS) with details of a potential project at Kaesŏng. Proposals were in the air for the construction of an 'industrial park' on the outskirts of the city, which had been the capital of the peninsula during the Koryŏ period (AD 918–1392) and which since the end of the Korean War had fallen within the boundaries of the DPRK. Although the 'industrial park' was to be located outside of the historic limits of the city, Dr Michell was concerned that within the 3,200 hectares to be developed, it was very likely that archaeological sites would be at risk from the construction of the park and that provision should be made for rescue archaeology ahead of the development.

At the same time it was felt that as a result of the necessary relaxation of border controls attendant on the construction and operation of the park, an opportunity might present itself for the development of heritage tourism within the historic limits of the city.

The role of the Museum of London lay in the provision of specialist advice in regard to archaeological investigation (in the industrial park or the city as necessary) within a commercial environment and under 'rescue' conditions—a situation in which MoLAS has thirty years of experience. As time progressed, the potential contribution of the Museum expanded to include advice on the preparation of World Heritage Status documentation, the presentation of historic sites, and the recording of vernacular architecture, amongst other things.

Potential

At its height Kaesŏng had over a million inhabitants; it was the national capital for 400 years; known monuments include two dozen royal tombs, a royal palace and an academy devoted to the training of Koryŏ state officials; it had a thriving trade with China and may have played a major part in the development of ceramic and printing technology. The shrinking population of the city has meant that many archaeological sites lie undisturbed by modern development, opening up numerous possibilities for the investigation through archaeology, coupled with a re-reading of many written sources, of the social, economic and political development of the city and its hinterland.

Two reconnaissance trips were made to Kaesŏng with a view to gaining some insight into the current state of knowledge about the archaeology of the city and its hinterland, whilst at the same time assessing the practical aspects of undertaking an archaeological project many thousands of miles from the Museum of London's normal base of operations.

First reconnaissance, January–February 2003

At the invitation of the DPRK tourist authorities and with the assistance of the National Bureau for Cultural Property Conservation and of the Kaesŏng People's Committee, a trip was arranged to Kaesŏng in late January 2003. The party was led by Dr Michell and included the author, Dr Elisabeth Chabanol of the Ecole Française d'Extrême-Orient (EFEO), Tineke D'Haeseleer, a research student working on Chinese texts pertinent to Kaesŏng, and two journalists from *Time* magazine.

Following arrival in Pyŏngyang, a couple of days were spent acclimatising to the sub-zero temperatures (minus 12 degrees C on arrival) and visiting the Korean History Museum, the Folk Museum and the fortress hill of Moranbong in historic Pyŏngyang before moving southwards to Kaesŏng.

The emphasis on arrival in Kaesŏng lay in visiting the sites for potential archaeological intervention and in meeting local archaeologists in order to gain an overview of current knowledge and capabilities. Despite some useful time spent at local monuments, these intentions were less than wholly successful, largely owing, it seemed, to an unwillingness to engage in unscheduled interviews on the part of DPRK officials. Although a number of substantial monuments could be visited—the Manwŏldae palace, Kongmin's tomb and Namdaemun gate—there seemed to be little or no attempt to present information about or interpret these sites or a coherent understanding of the historic city as an entity in its own right, still less of its place within a wider landscape.

It was perhaps not surprising that the monuments were treated as individual

Fig.1. Kongmin's tomb and environs (© David Lakin/MoLAS)

entities and the presentation of information was relatively sketchy. However, it was clear that considerable time and effort had been expended at some sites, most notably at King Wang Kŏn's tomb, to renovate the structures—although the effort was clearly largely directed at producing an 'as new' effect, which might not meet the most exacting of standards of historical authenticity.

The Koryŏ Museum, accommodated in the former Confucian academy of Sŏnggyungwan, had a representative selection of material relevant to the period of Kaesŏng's heyday, but little attempt had been made to put the material in context. It was not possible to visit the reserve collections for the museum and it was by no means clear how extensive these were or where they were held.

Second reconnaissance, August 2003

Dr Chabanol and the author made a return trip in August 2003 in somewhat more clement weather for a further reconnaissance, at the end of which a memorandum of understanding was signed between Euro-Asian Heritage Development (EAHD—Dr Michell's company) and the National Bureau for Cultural Property Conservation

Fig.2. Re-erected pagoda in the grounds of the Koryŏ Museum (© David Lakin/MoLAS)

(hereafter Cultural Bureau). The memorandum was the result of a further series of visits to monuments in Kaesŏng and its environs. The principal proposals were:

- Kongmin's tomb: non-invasive survey of the queen's tomb to establish whether its contents had been 'looted' in the colonial period; topographic survey of the associated monastic enclosure; development of a visitor centre/site museum
- Manwŏldae palace: trial excavation, topographic and other non-invasive survey concentrating in the western part of the complex
- Kyŏngdŏk palace in Kaesŏng: a hitherto unexcavated aristocratic residence thought suitable for trial excavations

The site visits were made in the company of Professor Jeon from Kaesŏng University. He was a very useful source of anecdotal information about previous field work at these sites. Regrettably, however, no original records were made available for study and, despite an agreement to provide access to these, none have yet turned up.

Activity since August 2003

Euro-Asian Heritage Development Corporation in association with the EFEO have recently developed a further proposal for trial excavations at the Namdaemun gate. Severed from the line of the defences as a matter of policy in the colonial period, it now sits in the middle of a traffic island.

Kaesŏng has a major heritage resource in the 1,800 or so vernacular buildings surviving in the centre of the modern city. These represent a fraction of the number which would have existed in the heyday of the city. They are nonetheless likely to come under threat of demolition as an economic upsurge propelled by the development of the industrial park brings both cash and people to Kaesŏng. EAHD seeks to preserve

Fig.3. Outer door to house in central Kaesŏng (© Euro-Asian Heritage Development)

Fig.4. Traditional houses in central Kaesŏng (© David Lakin/MoLAS)

these buildings as part of a heritage zone which would serve in part as a tourist resource—hotels, restaurants, etc.—and in part as a living history museum. The aim is to refurbish these buildings and encourage the current residents to take up the employment opportunities created in the heritage zone. The Folk Hotel, Minsok Yŏgwan, in the historic area has recently been acquired by a Korean Australian and is being refurbished.

EAHD has signed an agreement with the Cultural Bureau to develop the museum shop of the Koryŏ Museum, which includes training craftsmen making souvenirs and developing the area to provide income to support the museum.

Hyundai commenced construction work in the industrial park in the summer of 2005, and a team of South Korean archaeologists have made discoveries. Only anecdotal evidence for this has filtered through to the author, but it seems as though the discoveries include both pre-historic and Koryŏ-period sites.

Conclusion

With the realisation of plans for the industrial park coming on apace, the risks to the historic remains of Kaesŏng resulting from the consequent economic upsurge are increased. Unplanned development is likely to result in the destruction of archaeological sites, both inside and outside the historic city, as well as of many of the surviving vernacular buildings in the historic core. Increased visitor numbers are likely to degrade even protected monuments if not carefully controlled.

It is particularly important that a management plan for the heritage of Kaesŏng be implemented while there is still time. Happily the DPRK authorities are currently in the process of preparing a World Heritage Site application for Kaesŏng. It is to be hoped that this will provide a suitable framework for protection and development of the quite remarkable heritage potential of Kaesŏng.

BAMBOO CURTAIN OR OPEN DOOR? CHALLENGES AND OPPORTUNITIES OF THE DPRK: PERSPECTIVES OF A BUSINESS CONSULTANT

KEITH BENNETT

Perhaps it is invidious to pose my title in the form of a question: bamboo curtain or open door?

It is not that it is always impossible to establish the truth about the Democratic People's Republic of Korea (DPRK). It is more that, having arrived at the truth, one is more than likely to conclude that the opposite is equally true. As Bruce Cumings, especially in his book *Korea's Place in the Sun: A Modern History* (1997), has explained, probably better than any other author, the DPRK cannot be understood separately from the whole history of the Korean people.

I once heard Dr J. E. Hoare, who in 2001 opened the first British Embassy in Pyongyang, put it well. Speaking to the first—and, regrettably, so far the only—trade promotion delegation from the United Kingdom to visit the DPRK with the official support and sponsorship of Her Majesty's Government, he suggested to the delegation on their first night in Pyongyang that: "Koreans can be somewhat cussed people. If they were not, they would have become Chinese in approximately the fourteenth century." Koreans' behaviour, their self-perception as a nation and a people, has been forged in the belief, by no means misplaced, that they have had to wage a tenacious struggle not to be swallowed whole by their neighbours and other external powers.

Kim Il Sung's assertion, that one cannot properly understand and interpret the DPRK without taking this belief into account, was forged in the days of Korea's colonisation by Japan and of the resistance to that brutal colonial experience. It was against this background that he created his worldview of *juche*. Usually translated into English as 'self-reliance', it is better understood as trying to convey the raising of independence in every sphere of national life and society to the level of ideology.

To offer a contrast to this view, or to refute it, by reference to the very substantial aid and assistance received from the former Soviet Union, Eastern Europe and China over past decades, or from the World Food Programme and other humanitarian bodies, China, South Korea and others in the international community in the last decade or more, misses the essential point—at least so long as one's aim is primarily to understand the Korean mind-set. The establishment of juche is the goal, and any means or method is acceptable in the service of its ultimate realisation. Hence North Korea can be more flexible, at least in certain areas, a couple of which I will touch on, in the terms and nature of its openness to foreign business partnership than other Communist, and even some post-Communist or non-Communist economies, whilst also being considerably more rigid in many other areas.

Or, to put it another way—it is a case of both the open door and the bamboo curtain.

The DPRK's economic record

In looking at why investors or foreign businesses might want to take an interest in the DPRK, the first point to be made is that the country has by no means always been a basket case.

For the Japanese, Korea had two pressing advantages as a colony: it was the door to northeast China and the Asian mainland; and it possessed abundant mineral resources. Their approach may have been extractive and exploitative in nature, but the Japanese built mines to get at the resources and railways to get them to port and thence to Japan.

The post-war division of the Korean peninsula left the mountainous north with a perennial problem of how to ensure sufficient food for its people. But that same inhospitable terrain was, and remains, home to an abundance of minerals and raw materials. The successful exploitation of these resources was able in the past to provide the basis for a fairly comprehensively industrialised society, and their rehabilitation through investment could yet sustain the redevelopment of the DPRK's economy. It was largely on this basis, and for a considerable time after the armistice ended the Korean War in 1953, that the North developed more rapidly than the South, and radical economists and intellectuals in the third world, and a few beyond, professed to see a distinctive North Korean model of development that was, at least in certain respects, worthy of emulation.

Estimates vary as to when the deficiencies and limitations of a primary emphasis on heavy industry, based on a rigid form of central planning and relying overwhelmingly on these natural resources, became manifest. J. E. Hoare and Susan Pares, in their book *North Korea in the 21st Century: An Interpretative Guide* (2005) write that problems began to emerge in the mid-1960s. And, with the benefit of hindsight, they may well be right. Nevertheless, to my admittedly untrained eye on my first visit to the country in 1983, such problems did not seem apparent. Nor, I would say in my defence, was I alone. Whilst, recently liberated from the Cultural Revolution, Chinese friends would bemoan Kim Il Sung's, to them inexplicable decision to nominate his son as his successor, labelling it 'feudal socialism', in terms of the economy, it was not unusual in China of the early 1980s to see North Korea as something to be aspired to. Hu Yaobang, in many ways the most liberal leader of the Chinese Communist Party, repeatedly said that, in terms of socialist construction, North Korea had done a better job than China.

So the near collapse of their economy in the early 1990s, with all its attendant and related problems, the revolutionary changes among their erstwhile allies, the death of Kim Il Sung, the cruel succession of natural disasters, the decision not only to develop business relations, but also to solicit humanitarian aid from the 'imperialist enemy', must cumulatively have come as a severe blow to many, not only materially, but psychologically too.

Practical aspects

Let us look at some of the practical aspects of the question we have set ourselves.

Many people's first response, when the idea of doing business with the DPRK is put to them, is to ask: "Is it possible to do business with (or in) North Korea?" And: "Do the North Koreans want to do business?" The answer in both cases is: "Yes".

This may be attested to both by the case studies of actual and successful business that do exist as well as in the field of legislation.

North Korea passed its first law to govern the operation of joint ventures in 1984 and has successively added to its body of legislation to govern foreign investment and related activity year on year, especially since the early 1990s, with regard both to the succession of special zones that have been created in different parts of the country, and for the country as a whole. The body of legislation that presently exists is far from complete, but it is considerably in advance of what many people expect to find and is generally considered to be reasonable and practical in its tone and content. Moreover, once trust has been established, it seems to be increasingly the case that relevant North Korean officials are prepared to accept the need for help from their foreign partners in further improving the legislative framework and in preparing contracts.

Certainly, in my experience, nearly all foreigners, from even remotely relevant circles, be they banking, financial, academic, political, or whatever, will now be asked: "Can you provide training for our people?" North Korean officials have crossed that all-important threshold where they know what it is they don't know. Their desire to learn about all aspects of a market economy—amongst other topics—is very real.

One area of genuine frustration for the North Koreans is their inability, owing to financial constraints and a lack of support, to send more than just a very tiny number of students to study in the UK. It seems to me unfortunate, and a completely missed opportunity to promote gradual change and foster long-term goodwill, that our government currently seems determined to view North Korea solely through the prism of the nuclear issue and human rights, as important as these issues undoubtedly are, and will not make even a modest gesture in the direction of enabling more North Korean students to study in the UK and to interact with our banks and financial institutions.

As mentioned, there are a number of areas where, whether by virtue or necessity, North Korea may actually be said to be more open than either China or South Korea.

The legal procedures to establish an office of a foreign law firm in North Korea are much simpler than in China. Two have already opened and at least one more is in the pipeline. Until now, South Korea has completely prohibited foreign law firms from setting up on its territory and is only now retreating from that position under World Trade Organisation pressure and in the context of the negotiation of Free Trade Agreements.

Majority foreign ownership of banks is still impossible in China, but there are two majority-foreign-owned banks in Pyongyang, both involving British capital and both where the foreign party has 70 per cent ownership. (Of course, it is true that the scale of banking activity between the two countries is minimal, but nevertheless the principle has been established.) Although they are strictly off limits to North Korean nationals, the DPRK boasts two casinos, one owned by Stanley Ho in Pyongyang and one by Albert Yeung in the Rajin Sonbong Free Economic and Trade Area in the northeast, which was established in 1991. No such legal venture would be allowed on the Chinese mainland.

The small British oil company Aminex, listed on the Alternative Investment Market and on the Dublin stock exchange, has, on extremely generous terms, been granted exclusive exploration and exploitation rights for onshore and offshore oil and gas exploration, based on production-sharing agreements.

North Korea is happy for businesses to operate 'below the radar', such as British American Tobacco's two cigarette factories. Although hardly a top secret to those familiar with the North Korean business scene, this was reported as an 'exclusive' in the British press in October 2005.

In passing, it must be said that sometimes North Korean flexibility and openness can be ill advised and ill fated. Probably the most extraordinary example was the 2002 establishment of a special economic zone in the border city of Sinuiju, facing the Chinese city of Dandong across the Yalu river. This zone was to have a foreign governor, Yang Bin, a Dutch citizen of Chinese origin. Yang made a series of radical announcements: Sinuiju's existing inhabitants were to be shipped out en masse; the city was to have its own government, made up of a majority of foreigners, including Americans, as well as its own police force; it would have a visa-free regime. It would be a new Las Vegas. Incredible as it might seem, the North Korean authorities appeared to have omitted to consult China about these plans, which clearly held major implications for Beijing as well as Pyongyang. And even reading the *South China Morning Post* in the months before the Sinuiju announcement would have yielded the information that Yang Bin's luck was rapidly running out in China. Before he could make it to Pyongyang to collect his diplomatic passport, Yang was taken into custody in China, where he is now serving a 17-year sentence on financial and corruption-related charges. Despite periodic press speculation regarding a new appointment to fill Yang Bin's now vacant post, there the Sinuiju project has essentially remained until now.

Returning to more practical matters, I would submit that both parts of our dichotomy between the bamboo curtain and the open door can be equally true.

Getting to Pyongyang is not easy. Probably no other country is today served by just two regular flights per week, reliable, but in small, cramped and ageing aircraft. Likewise, it is probably the only place where, as a matter of routine, you may be required to surrender your mobile telephone at the airport, but where equally you can be sure of getting it back on departure. And, despite the frustrations of getting there, the nail-biting wait for a last-minute visa being one of them, it is also one of the few places in the world where you can feel almost completely safe and where, in contrast to Beijing, you can open your bedroom window and enjoy fresh air. Whilst the internet remains off limits, even to most of your business partners in Pyongyang, a much greater readiness and ability to communicate by email is making practical and ongoing communication much easier.

A more substantial problem, arising in part, but not exclusively, from the country's difficult economic conditions, is what we might call the psychology of business.

Despite the assertion that profit is officially no longer a dirty word, indeed, has been advocated in editorials of the Party newspaper *Rodong Sinmun* and in remarks attributed to Kim Jong Il, the notion lingers among many North Koreans that business is some sort of favour bestowed on the foreigner and its success is to be measured solely in terms of how much money is committed or, more often, pledged by the other side, without regard to the need for that other party to see a return, or at least the prospect of a return, on its investment. On a certain level, that is fair enough. After all, one presumes that the investor has not gone there simply to be charitable either. It's just that a little more subtlety might sometimes pay more dividends.

Besides the fact that the North Korean side is probably both chronically short of cash and under pressure to be earning some, the origins of this somewhat mendicant approach can also be traced, in part, to the situation where most of the DPRK's early joint-venture partners were drawn from the Korean community in Japan. Whatever the reason, 'patriotic donations' to the homeland have formed a considerable part of North Korean business activities. This has carried over into, indeed been compounded by, the economic fruits of the 'sunshine diplomacy' towards the North initiated by

President Kim Dae Jung in South Korea and continued by his successor President Roh Moo Hyun.

The clearest example is seen in the huge subventions paid by the South Korean company Hyundai Asan for the right to develop Kŭmgangsan (Diamond Mountains) as a special economic zone for tourism and the ongoing substantial payments which have to be made irrespective of visitor numbers and return on investment, leave alone the vast sum paid at least via Hyundai Asan before Kim Dae Jung went to Pyongyang for his historic summit with Kim Jong Il in June 2000. That such 'patriotic devotion' has not necessarily bought Hyundai respect or consideration can be seen in the strange case where North Korea threatened to freeze or scrap all Hyundai's projects after its chairwoman dismissed a key executive responsible for dealings with the North for alleged corruption. It is no surprise that the row was subsequently patched up. Inter-Korean relations have their own dynamic, and the North would certainly have been very reluctant to lose such a guaranteed income stream. More sobering was that this game was played out without any apparent regard for those in the international community who might be waiting and watching to see if North Koreans can make reliable and trustworthy business partners.

Summing up

Why should business people think about investing in or doing business with North Korea? On the negative side, they have to consider the criticism that they might face. They have to consider the threat of US sanctions and other obstacles that might be placed in their path, such as the US measures against the Banco Delta Asia in Macao, which forced it to cease dealing with the corresponding accounts and payments for North Korean banks and companies, after handling them for decades. The knock-on effect has practically frozen North Korea out of the international banking system. And simply, why go to North Korea when there is so much choice, when every country in the world seeks Foreign Direct Investment, and when North Korea is right next door to China, which is awash with opportunities?

Against that, as we have seen, there are areas where North Korea can be more flexible than China. Differences of scale can mean, for example, that those for whom the banking sector or the oil industry in China would be beyond their reach may be able to develop such businesses in North Korea. For other companies, which may be successfully operating in China or elsewhere in the region, North Korea can prove to be a relatively straightforward addition, to be administered from a regional office.

North Korea industrialised before China. In distinction to China's situation, the majority of its population is urbanised. In general, wage rates are the lowest in Asia, lower than those of China, Vietnam or Indonesia. And the legacy of the socialist system, whatever the negative baggage it has also left behind, has ensured universal literacy.

Moreover, the residual social welfare structure, even if rudimentary, inadequate and sometimes now honoured in the breach in areas such as housing and health care, which, despite the economic reforms introduced from July 2002 onwards, are still far from being fully marketised in North Korea, constitutes a practical support to the foreign employer, as well as to the local employee, by ameliorating to a certain extent the low wage levels.

Such factors can make North Korea an attractive manufacturing base to supply not so much the still very nascent domestic market as South Korea, China and the Russian Far East as well as Japan, once political tensions are lessened. If the Kaesong light industrial special economic zone being developed in conjunction with the South Koreans performs well, then there will be a very visible and practical illustration of this point.

Finally, and not least, far-sighted and adventurous businessmen understand the potential and long-term advantages and benefits of being the first in. Despite the tensions and high drama of the nuclear issue, China, Russia, South Korea and, in its own way, Japan, are all adamantly against a war on the Korean peninsula, and there seems to be no real appetite for it in the US either, especially after the Iraq debacle and the wider regional tensions in that part of the world. Difficult as it no doubt is, there really is no alternative to a peaceful, diplomatic solution.

A major component of that will be economic. It is not simply a matter of North Korea being paid off for renouncing its 'nuclear deterrent'. The international financial institutions will have a major role to play in rehabilitating the North Korean economy and bringing it to the point where reunification starts to become a viable proposition, rather than an intolerable burden on the South Koreans.

Such an eventuality will lead to major opportunities in just about every economic sector. As a prelude to a smooth process of reunification, one might envisage the creation of a Korean common market, in which North Korea would be an excellent manufacturing base as well, of course, as a major source of minerals and raw materials. Kaesong can be seen as the first example and step towards this.

However, for those who do business in Seoul the question of bamboo curtain or open door will remain.

THE VALUE OF INFORMAL DIPLOMACY AND CULTURAL EXCHANGES IN THE DPRK

NICK BONNER

Koryo Group

Since 1993, Koryo Group has specialised in travel to the Democratic People's Republic of Korea (DPRK) and in tourism and cultural exchanges with the country. The company has visited North Korea almost every month since 1993 and takes in around 70 per cent of all Western tourists to the country. In 2005, 700 tourists visited the DPRK with Koryo Group. It has been appointed as specialist advisor to the Korea International Travel Company, a DPRK government body, and has acted as consultant for the Lonely Planet guidebook and Bradt Travel Guide, which for the first time are opening the country to the wider world.

We believe that the tourist industry in North Korea should be encouraged. Tourism allows the Koreans to develop an understanding of the West, to train new guides and associated staff and to use English, all of which exposes the Koreans to the world outside and brings them into contact with Westerners, developments that otherwise might have been impossible. Tourism provides money brought in through legal channels. It requires the DPRK government to commit to a peaceful structure that interacts with the outside world. We have helped open up new areas and itineraries for tourists, which in turn improves contact with our Korean hosts. We push for local payment to provide finance directly to the local populace. Tourism has provided the access for several successful cultural exchanges—football friendship matches between amateur teams from Ireland, Holland and Hong Kong playing with North Korean teams, and school exchanges.

Working with the British film company VeryMuchSo Productions UK, Koryo Group has assisted in the production of two award-winning documentaries, *The Game of Their Lives* (2002), about the North Korean World Cup team of 1966, and *A State of Mind* (2004), which represented the first-ever access into family life in Pyongyang and the mass games. In 2004 and 2006, the company served as International Coordinator for the Pyongyang International Film Festival. With the support of the British Embassy in the DPRK and Ealing Studios, we have, amongst

Fig.1. A foreign visitor to the DPRK shares his snapshots

other films, screened *Bend It Like Beckham*, *Mr Bean, the Ultimate Disaster Movie* and *Bride and Prejudice* in Pyongyang. The films were seen by approximately 10,000 Koreans. We have also participated in music and travel programmes for British radio and television channels. A third documentary, *Crossing the Line*, that follows the life of Joe Dresnok, the last of the US military defectors still living in North Korea, had its world première in October 2006.

We believe cultural exchanges and informal diplomacy will have a significant impact in breaking down cultural barriers, as they have in the People's Republic of China. As in ping-pong diplomacy between the US and China in the 1970s, sports and cultural exchanges provide an opportunity for building relations and a stronger platform for human rights issues to be addressed. We have witnessed at first-hand the impact of cultural exchanges and from experience have seen they are a significant tool to engage with North Korea on a political and moral level that is currently under-utilised.

We accept that the North Korean government may use cultural exchanges as propaganda. However, the North Korean public are very much aware of the lack of information from the outside and that they are restricted in receiving it. Whilst engagement with North Korea is very strictly controlled, the lack of anything new in the country has given the Koreans an increased interest in the West. Cultural exchanges have a massive impact in a country where there is so little 'new' information leaching in from the outside world. Within this tightly controlled society there are individual Koreans who are willing to push at the edges—and they are very happy to work on cultural projects. We are in a very lucky position to have Korean friends who, whilst they have enormous constraints on what they can and cannot do, are prepared to push the limits.

The impact of football

We would very much like to develop football exchanges with North Korea and the United Kingdom, as this is where any cultural exchange would have the biggest impact. The Koreans love football and their teams are of a high standard. Their women's national team reached the 2003 Women's World Cup in the United States and their men's team performs well in the Asian championships. The love of football is a common bond on the Korean peninsula. Inter-Korean matches have been played over the years, and the success of the South Korean team in reaching the semi-final in the 2002 World Cup series (hosted jointly in the Republic of Korea and Japan) had a big impact, with North Koreans supporting the success of the South.

The DPRK is a country where the West is an abstract. Once there, the world you know does not exist. (September 11 and the 'end' of the Iraq war were not reported by the official media until a week after the events.) Football brings the outside world into the country. North Korea has one television channel during the week and an additional weekend television programme which occasionally shows international football. There is a thirst in North Korea for news of international football—even David Beckham is known there. In 1966, a cultural bridge was made between the DPRK and the West via the medium of football and the World Cup series. With VeryMuchSo Productions UK we conceived and arranged for the return of the DPRK 1966 World Cup team to the United Kingdom in October 2002. On the two occasions that the 1966 North Korean World Cup team came to England they were feted as heroes. The major impact of this friendship was in North Korea, where the public saw their heroes supported by the English fans and therefore changed many preconceptions that they had of the English. In the DPRK, the 1966 team refereed an informal match between the North Korean Foreign Ministry and a team drawn from Western embassies and aid organisations. In the UK, the ROK ambassador to Britain attended a reception for the North Korean team and met the players. In 2004, the 1966 team were invited by the British Embassy in the DPRK to attend the 2004 Queen's birthday reception.

Film productions

The Game of Their Lives

This documentary film centred on the North Korean World Cup team of 1966. They arrived in England as 2000 to 1 outsiders, but at the match in Middlesbrough in northeast England beat Italy, one of the favourites, and went through to the quarter-finals. Their arrival in the UK led to many political manoeuvrings. The British government did not want to give recognition to North Korea and succeeded in banning the playing of national anthems, apart from at the opening and closing ceremonies, and in permitting no reference to the 'DPRK', only to 'North Korea'. The team that came to the UK as the enemy and left having created a coup were embraced by the footballing world and above all adopted by the town of Middlesbrough.

No one believed we would meet the seven surviving players from the 1966 team, let alone be allowed to film, and that therefore we would have no choice but to cancel the project or raise the money with family and friends. We did meet the players and had enormous—in North Korean eyes unprecedented—access. For the first time Westerners had a glimpse into North Korean society. Allegations had been made in the West that the team had been disgraced on their return to North Korea and that they had lost their semi-final game against Portugal because of too much drinking and womanising. We were able to raise the allegations of player Pak Sung Jin's incarceration and of the 'womanising and drinking' and the arrest of the players on their return to their country. The film was a great success and received worldwide screenings. It was the first time a documentary had been shown in both North and South Korea. It won the Royal Television Society award and a 'special prize' at the Pyongyang film festival.

In October 2002, we took the players back to the UK. Funding was not

Fig.2. Ri Chan Myong, goalkeeper in the North Korean team of 1966, waving to the crowds at half-time at the Riverside stadium, home of Middlesbrough Football Club, October 2002. Over 30,000 fans gave the surviving members of the team a standing ovation.

forthcoming. We approached many potential sponsors but they were without doubt aware of the sensitivity of being seen as "supporting a rogue regime". Virgin Atlantic flew the players over in first class from China to Britain, but from then on the players had to look after themselves, with friends putting them up. Generous donations from individuals allowed us to rent the bus, pay for accommodation and meals and meet other necessities. A total of over 100,000 English football fans welcomed the players 'home' as they came on the pitch at Everton and Middlesbrough football clubs. The North Korean delegation travelled to Britain with a cameraman, and the resulting documentary they made was shown nine times in the DPRK. It was the first time that Britain had been portrayed in a positive light to the Koreans. It was also probably the only significant positive press North Korea has ever had in the West.

A State of Mind

Our second film was on the mass games that play such a prominent part in Pyongyang life. We thought we would get access to the mechanics of the mass games, but what we did not realise was the insight into North Korean society we would be allowed. The documentary was screened in both North and South Korea but on this occasion had a première at the Tribeca Film Festival in New York and a film run in the US. It has received critical acclaim. For many it confirms their pre-conceived ideas on the

Fig.3. Archive photograph of Song Yon, one of the gymnasts, and her family

control of the DPRK government, for others it also reveals the humanity of the people of North Korea. The North Korean criticism of our film was that it "was not as good as 'The Game of Their Lives' but was rather dull to a Korean because it was just like normal life." We could not have asked for a better criticism.

Crossing the Line

Our third documentary was started in May 2004. The world première was held in October 2006 at the Pusan Film Festival in South Korea. The film follows the extraordinary life of Joe Dresnok. In 1962, Dresnok, a US soldier, was posted to guard the peace in South Korea on the 38th parallel. At the height of the cold war, he deserted his unit, walked across the heavily fortified area dividing the two Koreas and defected to the North. The existence of an American defector was denied for decades by both the US and DPRK governments and only in 1996 did the US declare knowledge of Joe Dresnok and of a small group of other US defectors still living in the North. He became a coveted star of North Korean propaganda, and found fame acting in films, typecast as an evil American. He has lived in North Korea twice as long as he has in America. He uses Korean as his daily language and has three sons from two wives. This film was obviously more difficult to make than our previous two; nonetheless, the access we had was exceptional.

Fig.4. Film crew at the Joint Security Area, Panmunjom

We have never had our films or radio shows censored. The first time the Koreans see a film is when it has already been shown in the West. In all three films we have had this unprecedented access and broached sensitive subjects and in so doing have revealed a greater insight into North Korean society.

Need for official support

We believe grass-roots engagement should continue with the DPRK. Engagement with the common North Korean in our minds can only be beneficial. However, many of our projects are limited by the lack of finance and more importantly support. With government approval and involvement, the private sector would be much more willing to sponsor projects that would show the Korean people just what is happening in the world outside their borders.

North Korea has an isolationist policy and we believe that, as part of a balanced policy of 'stick and carrot' towards North Korea, Britain should promote cultural exchanges as a way of helping to break this isolation. Football is the ideal medium for this, to exploit existing sporting links between Britain and North Korea. It is the game the North Koreans love and it captures their imagination. Even small-scale football exchanges would expose hundreds, possible tens of thousands, of ordinary Koreans to foreigners and stimulate further interest in the outside world. We believe that it is especially younger people who the British government should be doing more to target, and it is the Korean's love of football where the greatest impact would be.

Appendix

Interview with Mr Kim Gyong Nam (father of one of the gymnasts) during the making of *A State of Mind* (VMS/KORYO/BBC)

> I've been interested in sport and the arts since I was young. When I was at school, I did a bit of gymnastics, and in football...since I couldn't kick the ball very well, so every time we played football at school I was goalkeeper. Whatever the West has thought up until now, we and the people of South Korea are one nation and are compatriots of the same bloodline. I think our fourth place in the men's football [at the] last Asian Games [held in 2002 in Pusan in South Korea] was a proud moment in the history of our nation. I recall the emotion of the 1960s when our footballers beat Italy 1:0 and got to the quarter-finals of the world cup. Looking at those two matches, I feel confident that if only the North and South were reunited and we played as one team, we would be superior to any team in the world. So just by looking at this match, you can see how for us, reunification is such an important issue for the future of our nation—as a people, such sports matches cause us to feel very strong emotions. Right from the preliminary matches, people watching the South Korean [football] players saw that they were trying very hard to win first place

Fig.5. Kim Gyong Nam, interviewed during the making of the film *A State of Mind*

[in the World Cup 2002]—we also saw it with our own eyes—you could tell just by the way they played. Every time we saw scenes of our South Korean players playing just as well as countries with a long history of football and scoring goals against them, we were delighted and felt a lot of national pride. Even though we were watching it on TV, we gave real applause whenever they scored a goal. You could say we felt as if we were playing together with the players.

Editor's note: This paper is based on an earlier text by Nick Bonner, who has revised and updated the written material and supplied all photographs.

CONTRIBUTORS TO *BAKS 11*

KEITH BENNETT is a business consultant dealing with the Democratic People's Republic of Korea.
Email: keith.bennett7@btopenworld.com

NICK BONNER is Director of Koryo Tours, based in Beijing, and works in association with VeryMuchSo Productions, based in Sheffield, UK.
Email: koryotours@mac.com

MARGARET DRABBLE is the author of seventeen novels, of short stories and of much non-fictional work that includes biography and literary criticism. Her most recent novel is *The Sea Lady*, published in 2006.

ANDREW KILLICK is a Senior Lecturer in Ethnomusicology at the University of Sheffield, with research interests in Korean music, especially developments in traditional music since 1900, and in musical theatre of various cultures.
Email: a.killick@sheffield.ac.uk

DAVID LAKIN is Project Manager at the Museum of London Archaeology Service.
Email: davel@molas.org.uk

SOWON PARK is lecturer in English at Corpus Christi College, University of Oxford.
Email: sowon.park@ccc.ox.ac.uk

KEITH PRATT is Emeritus Professor in the Department of East Asian Studies, University of Durham, and is the author of numerous books and articles on Korea.
Email: k_l_pratt@yahoo.co.uk

DON STARR is Head of the Department of East Asian Studies, University of Durham.
Email: d.f.starr@durham.ac.uk

CORRECTION TO *BAKS 10*

In the tenth volume of *Papers of the British Association for Korean Studies*, published in 2005, two papers carried colour photographs for which inadequate captions and credits were provided. The editor apologises for these omissions and seeks to rectify them here.

Inok Paek: 'Music of the Fatherland: The North Korean soundscape in the construction of Chongryun identity in Japan', *BAKS 10*:135-45.

All captions are correct, but the editor thanks Mr Min Honsok of Chongryun Yonghwa Chejakso for permission to reproduce still photographs from the 1986 (fig.3) and 1992 (fig.4) video recordings cited after the References at the end of Dr Paek's paper. The author and editor have made every effort to secure permission from RTV for reproduction of the four images from the RTV video recording of 2003 likewise cited after the References.

Jiyoon Lee: 'In the eye of the hurricane of change: Korean contemporary art of the new millennium', *BAKS 10*:95-105

Preferred names for the artists and correct titles for the art works reproduced in this paper are as follows:
Fig.1. Do-Ho Suh: *The Perfect Home II*, 2003.
Fig.2. Do-Ho Suh: (a) *High School Uni-form*, 1996; (b) *Some/One*, 2001.
Fig.3. Yeondoo Jung: (a) *Bewitched #2*; (b) *Bewitched #10*.
Fig.4. Atta Kim: *The Museum Project*.
Fig.5. Joonho Jeon: *Buyuhada* (Drift and Wealth)
Fig.6. Osang Gwon: (a) *Twins*; (b) *Death*.
Fig.7. Inwhan Oh: *Where a Man Meets a Man in Seoul*, 2001.
Fig.8. Duck-Hyun Cho: *'Entering the Yseokuk'* project excavation scene.

Permission to reproduce the images in this paper has been kindly extended by the following:
Figs 1 and 2. Do-Ho Suh: Courtesy of the artist and Lehmann Maupin Gallery, New York.

Correction to BAKS 10

Fig. 3. Yeondoo Jung: Courtesy of Kukje Gallery.
Fig. 4. Atta Kim: Courtesy of the artist.
Fig. 5. Joonho Jeon: Courtesy of the artist and Arario Gallery.
Fig. 6. Osang Gwon: Courtesy of the artist and Arario Gallery.
Fig. 7. Inhwan Oh: Courtesy of the artist.
Fig. 8. Duck-Hyun Cho: Courtesy of the artist.
Fig. 9. Bul Lee declined further involvement.

The author and editor apologise to the artists and agents represented for failure to secure permission to reproduce the above images in *BAKS 10* and thank them now for their generous co-operation.

PAPERS OF THE BRITISH ASSOCIATION FOR KOREAN STUDIES

Articles intended for future volumes of *Papers* should be submitted in both hard and digital copy, wherever possible, or as an email attachment backed up by hard copy. Please note that the editor uses PC format and prefers MS Word. Please state format and word processing package used on your disk and so far as is possible submit material in a form that will be compatible with PC format. Manuscripts should be typed, double-spaced throughout, on one side of the paper only, with ample margins and sequential page numbers. Articles should be written in English. Although we have no strict rules about length, contributors should remember that most papers are derived from conference presentations.

References in the text should be clearly cited and set out in full **at the end**. They should incorporate full details of author(s) and editor(s), of date and place of publication and of publisher, and of journal name, issue and page numbers, where applicable. **Please attach all notes in the form of endnotes, which should be indicated in the text with a superscript, or raised, number.** The editor can supply a short set of style guidelines; or contributors may use commonly accepted style manuals (Chicago Manual of Style; Harts Rules for Compositors and Readers, etc). We will endeavour to produce a common style in the *Papers*, but will respect professional differences, so papers in a single volume may have slightly differing styles.

Romanisation systems for Asian languages commonly accepted in academic circles should be adopted: McCune-Reischauer (or Yale) for Korean; Hepburn for Japanese; and pinyin for Chinese. Use diacritics for Korean and Japanese; also for other languages that employ them. If you cannot incorporate the appropriate diacritic into your text, please use a circumflex or other common accent to indicate it. All East Asian characters must be in Unicode. Proper names should follow preferred spellings only when they accompany the title of a book or article written in English. Where they are affixed to an article or book written in Korean, they should follow McCune-Reischauer or Yale romanisation and should appear without hyphen, e.g. Ch'oe Namsŏn. Proper names should be given in the East Asian order of surname followed by given name. In references, romanise Asian titles using the applicable system of romanisation as outlined above and give, where appropriate, a translation (use square brackets if the translation is not printed in the original). Use standard translations wherever available. In a paper making frequent use of Korean, Chinese or Japanese words (or other such words), please italicise the word only on first appearance and place it in ordinary roman typeface thereafter.